Dieter Duhm

Eros Unredeemed
The World Power of Sexuality

About this book:

In a direct and committed language, Dieter Duhm describes the state of love in our culture today. He places the unsolved issues of jealousy, free love, faithfulness, longing, impotence and morals at the center of the question of true non-violence and peace. From the experience of free love he develops new perspectives for a new way of living, where love between two people no longer excludes free love. He describes the philosophical and social basis for a culture in which jealousy is no longer a natural law, where sexual desires no longer have to be suppressed and where faithfulness between two lovers no longer breaks down because of a too narrow vision of love. "Knowing love" is the term he uses for the process of developing a culture without sexual repression, fear and violence.

About the author:

Dieter Duhm was born in 1942 in Berlin, Germany. He has a PhD in sociology, is an art historian, author and psychoanalyst. He is the initiator of the "Healing Biotopes Plan" – a global peace plan.

Beginning in 1967 he engaged in the Marxist left and became one of the leading characters in the students' movement. He made a connection between the thoughts behind the political revolution and the thoughts related to the liberation of the individual and became known through his book Angst im Kapitalismus [Fear in Capitalism] (1972). Around 1975 he began publically distancing himself from the leftist dogmatism and shifted to a more thorough human alternative.

In 1978 he established the "Bauhütte" ('Construction Cabin') project and led a three-year social experiment with 40 participants in the Black Forest in Germany. The theme of the experiment was to "found a community in our times" and it embraced all the questions of the origin, meaning and aim of human existence on planet Earth. The outlines of a new possibility for existence arose with the concepts of 'free love,' 'spiritual ecology' and 'resonance technology.'

In 1995 he founded the peace research center Tamera in Portugal together with the theologian Sabine Lichtenfels and others. Today Tamera has more than 160 co-workers. Dieter Duhm has dedicated his life to create an effective forum for a global peace initiative that can be a match for the destructive forces of the capitalistic globalization.

More information: www.dieter-duhm.com

ISBN: 978-3-927266-13-1
© 2nd edition 2014, Verlag Meiga
Original Title: Der unerlöste Eros, 1991, Verlag Meiga
Edited by Dara Silverman
Layout: Juliane Paul, Cover: Drawing by Dieter Duhm
Printed by Lightning Source Ltd. UK/USA

Contents

Foreword

I have written this book because it was inevitable. Sexual love had to be viewed and approached from another angle. It is the subject of our time, even if the slogans proclaimed about it sometimes sound different. The theme of sexual longing is the focal point of our inner thoughts and feelings. More people today suffer from a sexuality which they are unable to cope with than from environmental poisons. In whatever area I have been involved in life, whether in revolutionary groups of the student movement, in the emerging alternative movement of the seventies, or in my work as professor and therapist, in the end I always encountered this subject. Up to now, the attempts to solve it in communes or through experiments of free love have failed. The various therapeutic or spiritual approaches have not helped much either. The core of the problem is intrinsically linked to our daily thought and behavioral patterns. It therefore cannot be viewed or solved while at the same time maintaining these habits. People say that the sexual revolution is over. Inside of us however, it has really not yet even begun. The previous attempts were too disoriented and too emotional to lead to the center of the problem. At the beginning it does not have to do with revolution, but rather with recognition.

I have written this book for love, even where I have had to show its dark spots. So that such passages do not get too heavy, I have at times chosen a lighter tone. I hope that the book can be read and understood by all ages. If one does not understand everything immediately, it is not so important, since it will become clear later. I would like to demonstrate that there exists a realistic possibility for love between the genders which is free of disguise, fear and jealousy. I would like to encourage all of those readers and lovers who can follow this train of thought to find this possibility within themselves and to act upon it. If there is a future for us and our children that is worth living, then it is to be found in a new form of sensual love.

It is not necessary to read the book from beginning to end. One should begin at the most interesting point addressed in the table of contents. Those who find the negative balance in the first few chapters to be too much should not restrain from skipping these pages and instead begin by reading the more enjoyable aspects first. By doing so, no important theory will be missed, since almost every section creates its own context which is understandable without further explanation. Despite the gravity of the subject, I do not wish the readers of this book any new nightmares, but rather genuine hope and anticipation. Love is no longer a fairytale; if we understand it, we can make it come true.

I dedicate this book to all who love, to all who are on their way to new shores with hearts ready to love: all who are seeking true faithfulness which no longer forces anyone to lie. I dedicate it to the children who will come after us, to the animals and plants that need protection and to comradeship of the human being. I dedicate it to the peace workers who do not let themselves be distracted by over-hasty spiritual slogans and half-truths, but instead are ready to face the incorruptibility of life itself.

In the service of warmth for all that has skin and fur.
Dieter Duhm

PART I:

UNREDEEMED EROS – UNREDEEMED WORLD

So That's What It's Really All About

Most people are very diligent in their daily struggle against sexuality. They do their best to hide their fantasies and desires. They buy proper clothes, make a proper face and wear a proper hat. They speak about decent things, about where they went on vacation for example, about the weather, about good places to eat. Their secret desires at the swimming pool or in the bar are only revealed to their closest friends, if they have any. If they belong to the cultivated classes, then they speak about art or religion or psychoanalysis. They are as serious and deliberate as monks in those old monasteries, who got it on secretly and afterwards had to repress it even more for fear of being caught and punished. It is outrageous when you think about the effort we make to appear different than we really are in front of others. We play the same game, which we call "culture," "decency," or "morality." Couldn't we finally agree on something else? People feel obligated to conceal very essential things from one another. The whole of anthropology, which is the science of human beings, conceals the sex of humans just as an apple does its core. Strange things happen which do not fit into the normal picture. A professor's wife posthumously finds a thousand photos of nude female students in his drawer together with notes of exactly when and where he slept with them. For forty years she knew nothing about it. A woman took sedatives for years in order to remain faithful to her husband and suppress her nymphomaniacal desire for a thousand men. Someone sexually abuses young girls and it soon becomes known that he was the nice uncle from next door. One could continue on indefinitely with such examples. Every man and every woman knows what I am talking about. Up to now our daily world and our fantasy world have been two different things, one of which is shown and the other concealed.

Inner dramatic scenes take place here, in the minds of millions of young people and adults, across all classes and cultures of society, regardless of religious, political or moral affiliation. For the sexual inner life of a human being, it does not make any difference whether you are a member of the Green Party or the Republicans, whether you are Buddhist or Christian, whether you are a pastor or a businessman. Sometime or another we have all fought a heroic battle against our desires, and we have been defeated by them, be it only in our fantasy. Sometime or another we have all fought against these fantasies as well, in order to remain clean, and in so doing have got ourselves pretty "dirty." This is because the fight against our instinct is the source of the constant flow of oil that we pour into our secret fire.

Just to make it clear: I am not talking about our grandparents; I am talking about us. I am not talking about the prudery of the Victorian period at the beginning of our century, but rather about the sexual crisis at the end of the twentieth century. The so-called sexual revolution has until now changed very little in the basic structures of our feeling and thinking. There is still a closed seed dwelling in each of us. Whether or not this seed can be discovered and sprout depends upon the direction in which the human species develops.

Sexuality – A World Power

Sexuality dominates literature and film, tourism, advertising and car design. If we take into consideration its subconscious forces, effects, tentacles and seductions, sexuality could be viewed as permeating the entire body of a society in the same way that the most refined nervous system does. Everyone reacts to it, voluntarily or involuntarily. Sexuality is the number one superpower and is much more powerful than the US, NATO or any other human power structure.

If you look at or read a well-made pornographic magazine without immediately reacting with indignation, you may notice that your body experiences a kind of rush. What is it? Watching a sadomasochistic scene in a movie, you may be turned on by it, in spite of the initial shock. If you allow the excitement to build up for a while, you will notice that it somehow starts to get under your skin. Only a tremendous power is capable of moving you so strongly. What sort of power is this? If you abandon yourself to your most horny and "filthy" fantasies without deceiving yourself, you will notice that an incredibly strong current flows through your body. What kind of energy is it? It is a sign of boundless desire, of a life not yet lived and of a great and secret bliss which is suddenly thrown into our everyday life.

If, confronted with this longing, you do not fall back into old excuses and moral defenses, if you do not let yourself be fooled by psychological or therapeutic explanations, if the marching in step of the masses does not soothe you and if you are really determined to pursue this issue, then you certainly know something about the importance of sexuality.

In principle everybody knows it. But we are accomplices to a conspiracy in which all of us have consented to disguise ourselves. We would be putting our whole social existence at risk – marriage, reputation, job and social position – if we decided to be truthful about sexual matters. Imagine a teacher in a secondary school who comes into the teacher's room one morning and tells his colleagues about the fantasies he used to masturbate last night.

Or imagine congress meeting on the subject of abortion and a representative begins to speak about his sexual fantasies in order to set the stage for dealing with the issue in a truthful and humane manner. Imagine what would happen if a person somewhere on the social and political world stage were to begin speaking as a human being without a mask. His contemporaries would alternately blush and turn pale out of embarrassment. Until now sexual honesty has contrasted sharply with the outwardly projected way of life consisting of morals, science, religion, etc. Sexual honesty would promptly confront us with the most shattering of all realities: we would realize, in the face of our true desires and longings, that our sophisticated lives have something ridiculous and deeply hypocritical about them.

One of the perversions of our intellectual and cultural history is the phenomenon of sexuality which, although it permeates the whole of society with its bodily and emotional forces, has been banished to the private and intimate sphere of life. If society wants to prevent more people from being ruined by their inability to cope with their private lives, this error must be corrected immediately.

Everyone is moved by sexuality. It is therefore a public issue of the highest priority which, in any more or less responsible culture, must be seen and treated as such. It is of the utmost importance to the internal health of a society whether or not the sexual nervous system is to be kept in darkness, beneath and beyond public consciousness, or whether it is to be integrated consciously and openly into social life. As long as sexual energies are relegated to the domain of private fantasies, there will always be the danger of the dams breaking, because in the long run the natural power of sexuality will not allow itself to be shrugged off. In every society where sexuality is repressed, sooner or later an explosive mixture of sexuality and violence will develop and detonate with a horror that knows no limits. Crusades, inquisition, war and concentration camps have been the consequences of a society that is falsely programmed in the area of sexuality. Human history has been characterized by a cruelty that can no longer be ignored. This will remain if we do not create basic structures for sexuality without deception or repression, and for the transformation of sexual energies from violence into sensual love.

There are many political and New Age circles where such a loud silence about sexuality prevails that the internal struggle being fought in the name of suppression can hardly be overheard. There are other circles where the sexual issue is discussed endlessly. I have no idea whether or not anyone could profit from either of them. Discussions about sexual issues do not make any sense unless new experiences can be presented or are possible. And if such experiences were possible, there would really be no need for discussion. Every man and woman loves sex, if they can enjoy it without fear or humiliation. This fact does not need to be discussed. These discussions basically follow the pattern of the same old suppression and dogmatization they are meant to overcome. Some people make their dogmas out of marriage and monogamy, others out of free love or abstinence or the cerebral orgasm of tantra yoga… All such ideologies and dogmas, whether chauvinist, feminist or religious, are a futile struggle against the truth. As long as the dispute continues about whether couple relationships or free love are more "correct," I would prefer to abstain. In reality, there need not be any opposition or antagonism between the two. One grows out of the other. The only question is whether our courage and motivation suffice in getting us to act truthfully on the basis of our experiences. Here everyone must make his or her own decision – and friends can be very helpful here.

Sex is the number one issue. Perhaps this is true today more than ever, because of the failure of the sexual revolution. Every period has its own way of evading this issue. The first cries of sexual liberation had hardly faded away, the dawn of the student movement had hardly waned, and the media had already declared that the sexual revolution was over. But behind the fashions and masks of modern emancipation there is often horrible misery. The sexual state of emergency rages on. No revolution has yet been successful, let alone a sexual revolution, only new types of conformity have resulted. The sexual liberation of humankind is not a matter of a few years; it is an historical process. What started 25 years ago in a quite unfocussed way with the student revolt was simply a beginning, not a completion. The process itself, the emerging sexual liberation and transformation of humankind, has nothing superficial about it, as do yearly fashions and vanity fairs. Sexual liberation has nothing to do with taste or "progressive" trends, but goes far beyond it, as is true for all inner human developments.

The sexual issue is neither in nor out; it simply is. It is the most intimate focal point of our time, at least in those cultures and societies which are not directly confronted with urgent material needs or war. The attempts at sexual liberation made since Emma Goldmann's time (the beginning of last century) are the beginnings of an historic process, and there is no going back.

Eros and Apocalypse

The word "apocalypse" means both world catastrophe and spiritual revelation at the same time. We live in a virtual pre-apocalyptic situation. As a result of outbursts of violence, of the approaching ecological destruction of the earth, and of the potential for military annihilation, humanity is on the verge of global catastrophe.

Let us assume that a global combination of air pollution, poisonous gases and climate changes has led to a serious disruption of human breathing processes. Nobody can claim that such a scenario is unrealistic, given the present methods of ecological and military devastation. What else could we do, other than use all means at our disposal in order to be able to breathe freely again? When a basic need of the human organism is threatened, and when not just one individual is concerned, but all of humanity, then the disruption of this basic need is obviously issue number one.

Sexuality is a similar basic need. It is just as elementary as breathing and it can be disrupted in the same way as the breathing process in the above example. We do not need to discuss the question as to whether or not sexuality per se is the focal point of the world. The conditions under which we have lived up to now have made this the case. It will remain the focal point as long as it is not explored, accepted and fulfilled.

All wars of the past have given us an impression of what will probably happen if, given the choice between ruin and revelation, we do not choose revelation now. But what revelation? Not for John's revelation at the end of the New Testament. We do not need any more divine inspirations, our own understanding is sufficient, our retrospect of 3000 years of history, our perception of causal relationships is enough.

We are dealing with the paramount interrelation between outer and inner catastrophe, between ecological destruction on the outside and spiritual destruction on the inside, between external war and internal war, between psychosomatic decay of the human species and global decay of the biosphere. You only have to look at the bodies and the faces in the metropolises of the white race, in

New York for example, and compare them with those of the blacks in order to understand what is meant by psychosomatic decay. This species, which jogs through the streets on Sunday morning, will not continue to do it much longer. It may be true that they have constructed monstrous industries and high-tech systems of the most astonishing kind, they have launched rockets into space bound for Saturn, they have built self-guided missiles, and yet they have found no method to protect themselves and their species from inner disintegration.

Not long ago I saw a truck transporting cattle; they were so crudely tied up that the ropes cut into the cows' hide every time the truck went over a pothole. Humans will continue to butcher the environment, to destroy their fellow creatures, torture animals, beat children, burn people of other religions and vent their hatred on nature, as long as they do not achieve inner peace. And they will not find inner peace as long as they continue to rape love. They rape it through their hideously false morality, through their constant lies, through the splitting of Eros into marriage and brothel, through an outmoded idea of love and through a much too restrictive notion of fidelity. In fact they rape love through their entire social organization, which does not strive toward love, but toward power and profit. They finish off their rape of love by stubbornly refusing to accept and recognize the truth of these insights.

This entire worldwide process of destruction and self-destruction contains one strange component, which I have never completely understood, but which I have encountered again and again: Individuals are not even interested in freeing themselves from the system that ravages them. Despite occasional premonitions of the insanity they are taking part in, they cling steadfastly to their fate. I have always been amazed at these beings; I call them the "unshakables." Because of their sheer masses, these unshakables make up the heavyweight class in the worldwide fight against love. And children are always the victims of this fight.

In addition to the large-scale apocalypse under which the world is collapsing, there is also a small-scale apocalypse, in which a child's world collapses. The children are often left stunned by the strains of the parents' relationship. They sense the danger of being abandoned for the first time. Their heart's desires are left unheeded by the overburdened parents. They are swamped with presents and at the same time ignored. So the child puts up a fight, cries, attempts to win the attention of its parents, but the parents have no room left for sympathy. In the end, the child realizes that it is alone. This is the most silent and the most shattering of all forms of torment. The pain is at times so excruciating that no tears come. The world is made up of many millions of such individual destinies. As children we all experienced this, or at least something similar. It has happened to all of us, one time or another, that our whole world has caved in, be it during childhood, during puberty or later. Such a collapse always has something to do with disappointed love, lies and desolation. When the parents do not live together in sensual love, because they themselves came from an anti-love background, they pass their torment and their hopelessness on to their children. In this way the same structures of devastation are repeated generation after generation. I am not exaggerating. The multitudes of maltreated and abandoned children are not an exaggeration, but a reality.

The intellectual history of humankind reads like a gigantic effort to avoid the issue of Eros, to play it down, to trivialize it, to deny it, and yet to go on living. For no other cause have we invested more daring and finesse, more cunning and malice, more false morality and deception, than for the suppression of Eros. For no other cause have we built such beautiful cathedrals, devised such profound philosophies, and passed such cruel laws. No other sin has been so extensively punished, with such brutality, sadism and lust, as have been the sins of the flesh. After being stigmatized by thousands of years of punishment and violence, humans have become more than a little apprehensive in sexual matters. We no longer dare to show our desires or openly harmonize our lives with our sexual drives. We have given in, despite the fact that we behave as if we were free and sovereign individuals. One characteristic of Homo sapiens runs like a thread through all of history, through all our attempts to deliver ourselves from our self-made veil of tears, through all of our philosophic, religious and political systems: our capitulation in the face of Eros.

If we consider the programs and lifestyles which are being offered these days by spiritual, ecological or therapeutic groups, this impression will be confirmed in a new way. These programs do not contribute to a solution of the issue of sexuality and love; they do not even touch the heart of the matter, but instead make a cautious, macrobiotic detour around it so as to keep well clear of anything important. "How do we overcome war in love?" or "How do we end the sexual crisis?" are questions which are not asked here. But instead, "How do we make our lives bearable despite war in love and despite the sexual crisis?" Our attitude of resignation toward love and sexuality has in the meantime become so total that it is sometimes no longer regarded as such. People are shocked when it is openly discussed. And their shock is justified, since they do not see any other possibility. The more remote sexual satisfaction becomes and the more we are forced to renounce fantasies of love, the more we cling to those things in life which are attainable such as money and career, or sport and adventure, or to spiritual things such as art, philosophy and religion. I am of course not speaking as an anti-religious person, and I disdain neither sport nor intellectual pursuits, but as long as they are not linked to a positive solution of the sexual issue, all these things are relatively unimportant in regard to the central issues – and in regard to the destiny of the Earth, which for some time has been giving cause for concern and which appears to be coming apart at the seams.

There is a close link between the inner significance of Eros and the inner significance of apocalypse, or in other words: between the extent of happiness and satisfaction which is connected to Eros and the extent of general hopelessness and desolation which is connected to unredeemed Eros.

The following story appeared in the newspaper: A man meets a woman in Düsseldorf, a large city in Germany. They fall in love and drive to southern France. There they climb up a cliff, tie their wrists together and jump down. It was a honeymoon which had death as its goal. They wanted to be together forever. But the rules of society left them no other choice. They were certainly not insane, but rather seized by the overwhelming power of sexual love.

The search of the genders for one another has been the driving force of human history to present time; it has been the true passion of humankind. Love has always been linked to death, because in life there is no opportunity to turn it into a lasting reality. But what is it really, this thing that so strongly demands fulfillment and yet must remain unrealized? What inner concept of love and devotion can cause two people to choose death in order to avoid failure in life? What rupture has occurred in our world which leaves love in one place and life in another, and prevents them from coming together? Why has the most beautiful dowry of our lives turned into a source of eternal struggle instead of a source of eternal happiness?

The experience of sensual love is a key moment of awakening for both genders. Mind and body are suddenly aroused, as if they had previously been in a kind of stupor. We feel like we are reborn. This horny, healing and soothing energy acts on the center of our cells and organs. Sex, sexual love, desire and sensuality are aspects of an extensive organic process, which goes far beyond the physiological concept of the gratification of urges. After wonderful sex, we radiate like the morning sun, because we have just held the world in our arms and have come so close to the source. Likewise, a religious experience is not merely a spiritual process, but an organic one as well. The genuine healing process for any human being consists of these two fundamental experiences, namely the erotic and the religious. The same "principle of happiness" is valid for both processes – we are accepted, we have found ourselves! It's like a real homecoming, or a childhood dream when it comes true. There is an overwhelming feeling of joy and gratitude.

Sensual love between the genders is a primordial experience of bliss. It is one of the most archetypal images of our longing. It makes its presence felt in our childhood fairytales in an unconscious or dreamlike manner. It is even more feverish and foreboding in the bliss of first love. Out of the dreams and the aspirations surrounding this supreme joy arose poetry, the myth of the hidden treasure and the blue flower of romanticism. Nothing, nothing in our hearts can keep us from pursuing this path and this goal, as long as it somehow appears to be within reach. We are prepared to throw aside all our reservations and inhibitions if we see such happiness before our eyes, waiting to be grasped.

This is where we see an inner relationship between Eros and Apocalypse. Just as profound as the happiness which results from fulfillment is the pain which results when fulfillment is not achieved. Just as profound as the yearning in Mignon's song (Goethe) is the desperation, the rage, the destructive fury of betrayed hearts. The apocalypse has been in preparation for quite some time, it began where this desperation and destructive fury became part of general human structures.

Where it flows freely, love is the most profound and beautiful thing in this world. But when it is obstructed and betrayed, it is the darkest and ugliest thing in the world. The destiny of love is at the center of every individual life, for it is the center of all humankind. The painful drama of love that we experience firsthand, all of the many millions of us, for better or for worse, adds to the drama of all humanity. If we want a better future, then we need a new concept of love. I hope the thoughts contained in this book can contribute to finding it.

At this point I would like to say something fundamental that may help to clear up misunderstandings: When love is mentioned in this book, much more is meant than just sexuality. The sexual revolution, which is necessary for creating a humane world, can only take place if it is linked to an equally indispensable spiritual revolution. A new concept of love also contains a new concept of dealing with nature and all its beings. The complete liberation of sexuality can only occur in a spiritual context in which the principle of non-violence is understood and loved. The absolute equality of the genders, the healing of life and the care for all of creation belong to this way of living. The release of Eros will succeed to the same extent in which we are prepared and able to see and to put into effect these fundamental spiritual principles of an overall non-violent culture. There are cultural examples which can show us a lot, even though they originate in earlier times and cannot simply be adopted as such. I am thinking for example of the Hopi Native Americans culture and more significantly of the Bishnoi people in India. They have developed basic rules of life which are always valid when inner human healing is concerned, since this healing is always linked to a relationship of human beings with the rest of creation which is non-violent and thus free of fear. The complete liberation of sexuality is part of this relationship as well. As long as we continue to repress and deceive, we will have war in love, and as long as we have war in love, peace will be impossible on Earth.

There Can Be No Peace on Earth So Long as There is War in Love

It was a good sign that during the Gulf War hundreds of thousands of people took to the streets to demonstrate against war. But I am afraid that such demonstrations will continue to be powerless, as long as we have no concrete vision of peace and no conviction. And even the faintest promise of peace will remain unattainable as long as peace is lacking among us and inside of us.

In the famous tragedies of ancient Greece the battle of the genders already played a central role. Liz Taylor and Richard Burton, like all passionate couples of this derailed world, tirelessly continued to perform the old tragedies. When the passion has expired from the relationship, we are now too civilized to beat each other's heads in. Instead we go on a vacation to Rhodes, where we argue about what to take pictures of. One way or another, openly or secretly, the battle of the genders is rooted in misunderstood and unfulfilled sexuality, or absence thereof. This problem crosses through all layers of society, religious affiliations and other beliefs. The structure of the relationship between the genders, within which almost everyone lives today, contains a core of sexual disappointment and resentment, of bruised love and latent revenge. As long as this structure continues to exist, peace will not be possible among human beings, at best only polite agreements and weak compromises. Those fighting for peace cannot really believe in themselves anymore, as long as the daily skirmishes continue at home. I do not want to offend anyone, but isn't almost every marriage and almost every couple relationship a weak compromise, after the initial euphoria has worn off? There is no doubt that divorce statistics say enough about the necessity for a fundamental change of course. Is it really necessary for further masses of children to be made into emotional cripples, criminals and drunkards, before we give way to change? Will children ever be able to develop a positive association with the word peace when the necessary basic trust has been beaten out of them at an early age?

There is certainly no ready-made peace plan for this bloodstained Earth, in the same way that there is no ready-made program for love. But there are some aspects of the relationship between the genders which will definitely play a part in the decision as to whether war or peace shall prevail on Earth. Two of these aspects are to be briefly discussed here.

First: Will we succeed in building a human coexistence where sexual affections of one toward another do not invoke fear, jealousy and hatred in a third?

Second: Will we succeed in building a sexual relationship between the genders in which the woman can give herself up to her desires without fear of being scorned and humiliated by the man?

At a time where we are talking about politics of peace and an Earth without violence, we can no longer ignore these two aspects. They belong too much to the essence of a humane world. If they were to be completely fulfilled, the war of the genders would be over. Then we could begin with the concrete work for the Earth along the lines of a realistic vision. This would require a change of views from the human race as a whole, a change which would perhaps be the most profound since the decision to come down from the trees. Our intelligence would have to be turned away once and for all from serving war and won over for serving love.

High-Tech in War, Neanderthal in Love

To this day, Homo sapiens have invested their intelligence in war, not in love. Evolution researchers and neural physiologists have had serious worries that this could be a result of a brain malfunction. Humans, especially men, have wasted their libido on weapons, tanks, battleships and missiles, an indication that war turns them on more than peace. War is sexy. All disarmament agreements to date have failed because of this inextinguishable characteristic of the male psyche. The fervor with which war heroes perform their military strategy games surpasses, by several orders of magnitude, the lust with which they make love to their wives. Man, stuck in childhood, thus finds his use here, his meaning and his holy purpose. He does not yet know woman, because even as his mother she eluded him, all the more reason for him to cherish the sacrament of war.

The game of war is probably as old as man himself, having its origin in an archaic and Paleolithic impulse. When the Cro-Magnon man assaulted and exterminated the Neanderthal, he may have felt something similar to what Alexander's soldiers in Tyros felt, or the American soldiers in My Lai, Vietnam. Man is seized by an urge to destroy, which at times surpasses all other urges. And when the communists were leading their brothers to sunlight and freedom, their combat song ended with the cry, "Sacred is the final battle!", although they did not otherwise believe in anything holy. Love was just as unattainable for man as distant poetry, but war was his oath and command. Sex was merely a physical necessity, the canon was a sacrament. If in the course of history man had taken as much care of his wife and children as he had of his sword and canons, we would long ago have found the Garden of Eden on Earth.

Man has developed remote control projectiles, electronic defense systems and self-guided cruise missiles; here nothing seemed impossible to him. But where love is concerned, the same man snorts with jealousy, turns as red as a baboon or as pale as a ghost. On the one hand, men employ the most advanced technologies in planning interstellar war, but where women are concerned they resort to hand axes. Whereas the cerebrum is applied in war technology, in love man lives and thinks out of his spinal cord. Whereas in the game of war the rules are determined by discipline and farsightedness, in love all emotions are permitted. Without even giving it a second thought we employ two different standards here – a very high standard for war and a very low one for love. In the weapons industry the bar is placed at eight feet; in love most people fail to jump over the bar even when it is placed at only two feet, since they have learned that love is a matter of the heart and not something which can be the object of intellectual exploration. The fact that weapons technology and success in warfare are linked to research is obvious to everyone. But the idea that love could also have something to do with research and understanding lies beyond the prevailing Stone Age consciousness. Whereas they are prepared to go through the toughest tests of endurance in war, in love they seek the greenest pasture land to graze on. Whereas in weapon laboratories systems analysis and computer data processing are employed, we still follow the old fairytales when love is concerned. We should not attempt to fool ourselves here. The progressive dynamic sport shoe generation of today adorns itself with super-electronics and galactic hairstyles, but in their hearts they still dream the same fairytale dreams of our grannies. The cars and the changes in fashion have become faster, but serious reflection on matters of love has not.

If we want to create a transition from a period of violence to a new era of structural non-violence today, then we have to totally change our priorities. The same love and attention, the same conscientiousness and reliability, the same force of will and intelligence with which humans have thus far used to destroy each other must now be used to promote sexual love. We can no longer confront the omnipotence of war with white doves and pious songs. Our latent fascination with war and destruction is too great, too sincere and too profound, whereas our ideas and images of peace have so far been much too weak, immature and half-hearted. Not until we have found something even greater and more fascinating than warfare and power games will we be able to believe in the possibility of overcoming war on a global scale, and this something could well be sensual love based on friendship and solidarity and on a sincere, powerful and erotic relationship between the genders – in short, a true reunion of man and woman. The only kind of will power and intelligence which can enable us to thoroughly and permanently clear out the ancient martial nooks and crannies of the soul is one which is capable of creating the basic structures of a love life without fear and violence. Human beings that have sent rockets into outer space will also be able to solve the problem of unredeemed Eros if they fully dedicate themselves to this task with all their will power and intelligence. We must keep in mind the fact that the sources, energies and growth processes of creation are directed toward a true love potential which we can realize if we are aware of it. Processes of germination and growth, flow forms in water and the learning processes of a child show us something about the essence of life and love that can no longer be ignored. Life is boundless and limitless and without burden, it cannot be squeezed into preconceived, linear structures.

Done to Eros What We Did to the Rivers

.ve done to the rivers? We have done two things to them: we have pumped our sewage wastes into them and we have straightened them, both of which we have done to Eros as well. And in both cases we have achieved the same result: we have taken away the natural beauty and healing power that was originally present.

We have pumped our sewage wastes into the rivers and we have pumped our foul thoughts into sensual love. Our parents were outraged by sexual matters which, as I discovered, was because they themselves despised sex, they have defiled and degraded it with their flawed thoughts, and then they said it was the sex that was tainted, not their thoughts. They simply poured their own sewage, in the form of foul thoughts, into their sexuality and confused it with true sexuality. Continuing with our metaphor, they said the river is dirty, and were thus outraged by it, instead of seeing that they themselves had made it dirty. The sexual morality of "decent" people has always functioned according to this principle. And since all of these millions of parents, teachers, priests, etc. were never able to recognize their own tricks, this forgery has continued until today. They say, "That's filthy and disgusting," and do not notice that the filth only exists in their own thoughts. It's like pouring hydrogen sulfide in your coffee and then afterwards complaining that the coffee has a fart-like smell to it. By such diligent and persistent reversal of the facts it is clear that you will eventually observe the phenomenon that is known as a "self-fulfilling prophecy." When it is claimed that sex is vulgar and dirty – for example sex without heart, sex without love, sex only for lust, sex as a purely physical urge – in the end that is what it becomes. For no human being and no sublime stirring of life, no love and no natural desire can preserve its beauty when it is continually forced to hide itself.

All energy has its natural flow, its natural direction and its natural rhythm. This applies to the energy of water and to the energy of sexual love as well. If we disrupt the natural flow, we cause disorders in the overall functioning of the organism in question. If we disrupt the natural flow of a river, we can expect corresponding disruptions in its biotope. Rivers follow the energy of water and its natural and oscillating movements as it flows through the landscape. This oscillating and meandering nature of water provides the river with its momentum and the power to cleanse itself; it endows the water with its healing capacity. Human beings, men in particular, orient themselves bravely and vertically according to the linear elements of life and perceive swinging elements as disruptive and resistant. They have straightened out the rivers and placed them in pretty little concrete basins. With this present they have destroyed and polluted the rivers, robbed them of their self-cleansing power, wiped out their biotopes, and poisoned the natural arteries of the Earth.

The concrete bed is to the river, what marriage is for Eros. We have interfered with the organic processes of nature in exactly the same way and "straightened out" the situation – we have relieved it of all its swinging fluctuations, its sidesteps and its waves of joy. Eros swings and dances like the water of a river. The water flows to the right, it flows to the left, it flows backwards, then it whirls around and flows in another direction, but it is always the water of the same river. We can always rely on this water, its healing power, its suitability for drinking and its transparency, as long as we do not disrupt it. We can rely on the potency of love as well, its warmth, its charm, its beauty and its healing power, if we do not disrupt it. But we must not try to fasten it and restrict it to a single person. We must not dictate to love what it may do and what it may not do, we must not force it to conform to our own egocentric desires, and above all we must not reduce it in order to make it fit into our own little world. If we make its bed too tight as in the case of the river, sooner or later it will forcefully break the dam. As it is often written in the newspapers, it happens that "conventional family fathers and respectable colleagues" suddenly have "unexplainable" bursts of hatred, murderous blowups or are involved in other acts of violence.

Bertolt Brecht asked the question: which is more violent, the current of water that breaks through the floodgates, or the dams that restrict the water? Which is crueler, the act of violence of a ho runs amok, or the moral law that compelled him to

A non-violent ecological culture will restore to nature its own forms of motion, to the river its meanders, to all creatures their wildness and to love its dancing. It will be a great journey of discovery, because everything, including the so-called dead matter, contains a strong impulse to move. You only have to take a thin piece of sheet metal as an example, cut it open and it uncoils with a sudden movement. The world is full of motion. Theodor Schwenk wrote a very informative book on the subject called The Sensitive Chaos which also includes many good pictures. Do we want to continue excluding the energy of sensual love from the universal dance of energies? Do we want to continue cementing it into claustrophobic marital cages and play dead in its sterile riverbed?

Eros and Religion – The Observance of Origins

I do not want to tie myself down to using any nitpicking terminology and jargon. But it may still be a good idea to differentiate between the overall theme of Eros and the more limited concept of sexuality, in order to focus on the all-encompassing human issue of our time and to avoid reducing ourselves to discussing relationship problems and sexual inadequacies. Whatever moves and touches the inner parts of our love regions has to do with our whole existence. I am going to attempt to make an outline of this overall vital space using the two concepts of Eros and religion, because that is where we can find the sources of our being.

Eros is veiled and shrouded sexuality. The essence of Eros consists of veiling and unveiling. In essence, veiling and unveiling are basic erotic processes which simultaneously conceal and reveal a mystery. The veiling of Eros was not originally meant as suppression or concealment, but rather as an uncovering and revelation. The veiled woman "waits" for the moment of her unveiling. She does not remove the veils until the time for it has come. The veiling of Arab women originally served the preservation of erotic knowledge as well, which was not divulged until the moment of revelation. In this way the woman "preserves herself" for the encounter with the man. This is not only about a misogynous custom; it is about a profound appreciation of Eros and a genuine idea of its true meaning. It is as if you had dreamed of something essential for quite a long time, something that you cannot relinquish so easily. The chastity, which is implicit in the veiling, is not an indication of false morality or inhibition, but rather an immediate spiritual expression of an erotic process which is just taking form. It is like an unconscious memory of a paradise which is veiled as you approach it and is not unveiled until you reach it. These are the deeper aspects of an emerging sexual morality, aspects which it then loses until it even resists the fulfillment of that which it was actually intended to prepare and protect. The intentional veiling is transformed into the moral "no" and the longed for unveiling is transformed into "sin." In this way, the whole process is disjointed from its erotic foundations. Sexuality without Eros comes into being, denudation without veiling, bareness without paradise regained. Sex, which originated in the unveiling and revelation of Eros, has been reduced to the gratification of a physical urge. We are ashamed, even if we do not notice it anymore, because we instinctively sense that we are doing something that does not genuinely correspond to the erotic and spiritual essence of sexuality. We cannot take sexuality for granted in the same routine way that we do brushing our teeth. To regain this knowledge in all its depth, without false mystification, is the demand that life and sensual love place on us today.

What we have here is a Babylonian language and thought confusion which, in the wake of the so-called sexual liberation movement, has not been reduced but instead substantially increased. Free sexuality, as put forth in this book, has nothing to do with mechanical unveiling, forcefully overlooking shame or forbidding authentic chastity. There are strong, authentic and even necessary reasons for occasional shyness and chastity. Free sexuality is the rejoining of sex and Eros on a new plane, which truly frees us from sensual banishment. By consciously putting into practice the rejoining of sexuality and Eros we begin a journey which leads simultaneously toward our destination and toward our source.

True Eros, like true religion, is linked to the origin of all things. Where human beings have experienced this origin, they have preserved and protected it by developing cultic rituals which remain closely linked to the original meaning. From this instinct arises the organic solemnity of a life ethos which is later transformed into external morality. But this morality, which I am compelled to unmask so vehemently in the following chapters because it has deteriorated into nothing but lies, did not originate from simple human arbitrariness or malice, nor from the power hungry priest mentality in Nietzsche's Genealogy of Morals, but rather from a primordial concentration on the sacred aspects of human existence. The holy observance of the genesis of human kind is the real motive behind all erotic and religious cults. If we consciously throw the old moral ideas overboard today, then we are not doing it in the sense

of an anarchistic rebellion against traditional cultural
rather in the service of a rediscovery and birth of the ̖
powers of life.

In order to achieve this we do not need to veil ourselves, nor do
we need to be ashamed of our "bashfulness," because the inner steps
of development in sensual love cannot be passed over by force. The
following explanations are thus no call for manifest emancipation,
but rather for the understanding of our sexual longing.

——— Jan 31

A few simple sentences about the subject of religion will suffice. The
reader will have noticed that the ideas expressed in this book go far
beyond a mere psychology of sensual love. If we want to straighten
things out for ourselves, it is not about mending failed love
relationships, but rather about resituating the issue of Eros within
our overall existence. In this way we involuntarily touch upon the
meta-psychological and religious core of our existence. The spiritual
anchor point of genuine love relationships is not only found in the
relationship itself, but in a certain comprehensive relation to the
world as well. As soon as an inner link with creation is sensed or
becomes conscious within the relationship, then I am talking about
religion. It is beyond all confessions and has nothing to do with
the church. The church as an institution is for true religion what
marriage is for Eros: a societal mechanism for the banishment and
regulation of the elemental forces of life, both sensual and spiritual.
We are living in a time when these traditional corsets that constrain
body and mind have begun to crumble and allow the real sources
of power to trickle through again. In spite of all the entanglement
and devastation we are coming closer to the source. The historical
double meaning of apocalypse is being fulfilled; step-by-step it is
turning into a conscious experience of revelation. The "Kingdom of
God on Earth," the sexual and spiritual power of love, can no longer
be confined behind society's masks, dogmas and institutions.

Sexual and religious love are the sources of our existence. We
cautiously approach them until they finally are one. In the course
of history the emerging human being separated them from one
another, which has been the cause of our permanent suffering.

Now, with the liberation of sensual love, we can reunite them and recognize the happiness in this union that we have unconsciously sought after for so long: the happiness of having achieved. This is the inner process of recognition of our time, the process of an approaching transformation of the life of humankind.

The cultural epoch of patriarchy fought against Eros by fighting against women. But where the seductive power of the woman has diminished, the man has also been left desolate – in religious aspects as well. He robbed himself of his own life source by domesticating her and forcing her into a regulated system of sexually hostile constructs. In doing so, however, he lapsed into a state of suffering that he was unable to overcome with his constructs, because all of his spiritual pain was so deeply linked with the pain of separation. Man lived in a disjointed world, separated from woman and separated from creation. The sacred, however, which is the object of all spiritual and physical desires, is still intact and undivided. Sensual love, like religious love, is an elemental experience of reunion and true redemption which is inherent in the overcoming of the separation.

Walter Schubart, in his fascinating book Religion and Eros, spoke of the "mercy of love," which is present in the experience of fulfilled sensual love. It is the authentic moment where sensual love, religious love and compassion come together. It is a condition in which all hatred and resentment dissolve. It is equivalent to a genuine energy conversion in the core of our organism. It is a jubilation of cells which have found their center and their source.

Goethe's figure Torquato Tasso praises the liberating power of lovers,

"*I feel changed in my innermost regions.*
I feel relieved of all affliction,
free as a god,
and for all I thank thee."
~ Johann Wolfgang Goethe, Torquato Tasso

When the lover stops clinging to his beloved as tightly as he clings to God, when he finally stops making this mistake and begins to release his grip on him or her, when he realizes that there are other laws that apply here which can liberate him, and if he follows these laws, then he can begin a steady progression to the source. The erotic experience is then no longer a sacrament that he closes, but rather a sacrament that leads to the most profound opening.

Every act of love that occurs in this manner is a service to the world, and it requires no marriage rings. God no longer exerts a foreign power over us or outside of us; we create God through our acts of love. Eros is the beginning of all things; it is both the place and cause of their creation. The erotic experience of men and women has a common origin, which the world religions have persistently attempted to obstruct. All true religion, however, is the discovery and observance of origins.

The deepest knowledge that can be gained through the contemplation of religion and Eros is found in the liberation of sensual love.

Free love is not a human invention, but rather a product of creation. The extent to which we become aware of these facts on a new level is the same extent to which the sacrament of marriage is transformed into the sacrament of free love. The sacrament of marriage was the first step in a chain of experiences which tracked down and recognized the religious depth of sensual love. It was in this respect much more than simply the apprehensive exclusion of others. It would not have become a sacrament if it had not been so closely related to the most basic erotic experience, where sensual love expands into love of humankind and love of god. Therefore our duty today does not only consist of destroying the old sacrament simply because it was too restrictive and too hypocritical. What matters to us is to understand what its intention was and to realize it on a new level. The basic values of love, devotion and companionship, which are prescribed by the institution of marriage, must be abolished and replaced by a new level of sensual and spiritual realization. Free love is not simply the destruction of marriage, but instead it takes up the same notion and helps to realize it under more clearly thought-out conditions.

The institution of marriage was probably introduced into western culture toward the end of the second century BCE through the Attic-Greek king Cecrops. It was meant to facilitate the integration of sexual life into a state that was not orientated toward love, because the concept of love we have today did not exist at that time. The development of free love on the other hand does not facilitate the subjugation of Eros under a state system, but rather its conscious reintroduction into the freedom of creation. By marrying into a certain family it was always possible for someone to become a respectable and acceptable member of society. Through free love we become members of the community of life and creation. The change of orientation from couple love to free love involves a shift in orientation toward a more comprehensive whole: it is not society or the state which is the focus of orientation, but life itself. The institutions of marriage and church are societal systems where life no longer fits in. Sexual love must no longer orientate itself toward these societal systems; instead new structures must be created which are orientated toward love. Free love will lead only to continual suffering in a society which rejects it. On the other hand, in the course of a non-violent restructuring of society, it will help to ferment the whole of human culture. This revolution cannot be achieved from the outside or by force, rather from the inside through the consolidation and reshaping of our real love relationships.

To conclude I would like to talk about a strange phenomenon which could be of utmost importance to those who choose the inner path of self-experience. Every true religious experience, even those which appear so novel to us and which make us so happy, are not simply new, but provoke a strong sensation of déjà vu within us. It is the very uncanny and surprising feeling that you already know the sensation. The unsettling and novel aspect of the experience is that it is familiar to us somewhere deep inside. We are simply left stunned by this sensation. "So that's what it is, that really exists!" We have reached the beginning and, like life, it is eternal. We know it already; we all originate from it and have experienced it often in various incarnations and spheres of existence. Now that this elemental experience of life has appeared again, we see that we have only changed stages and that we have experienced nothing that could be called non-human. We are filled with a nameless gratitude and look with amazement at that reduction of life which we have considered normality.

Exactly the same is true for the discovery of free love. Having awakened to a new potential of existence, we see images and thoughts which are as familiar to us as our most intimate feelings. We peer into the new regions of sensual love and with astonishment recognize the naturalness of the situation that we find there. People who love, who have overcome their fears, who have no more masks and no more fences! The world, which has been freed of its fences, is a love affair. As in the religious experience, there does not exist even the slightest doubt as to the reality of this "dream." It is like awakening from a film which has lasted for eons. And once again we are amazed at that reduction of life which, within the old structures of couple love and jealousy, we had accepted as "normality." The erotic and religious revelation is like a miracle, and the unexpected secret of this miracle consists in the fact that we already know it in our innermost experience. Ernst Bloch, in his momentous work The Principle of Hope, spoke of the "nondum" (Latin, "not yet"), the great unredeemed aspect of human history. In the erotic or religious redemption, we experience that it has, latently and unrecognized, always already been there. To make it reality does not require any acts of spiritual force or physical exertion, all we really need is the experience of love and truth in love. Then we will be capable of understanding what occasionally appeared to all of us during childhood and what still lies ahead of us in the form of a hidden goal and nondum: a HOME.

PART II:
THE SEXUAL ISSUE

Everyone Wants It, but What is It?

What is the goal of life; where does the journey take us? What is the deeper meaning of all the things that we do every day? What does our true fulfillment consist of, if something like that even exists? "My goal is to enter Nirvana," the noble one from the East would say. "My goal is to unite with Jesus," said Hildegard von Bingen. "The meaning of life lies in the recognition and acceptance of the predestined harmony," Leibniz would have said. Sonneberg, the brilliant artistic philosopher, wrote from inside the psychiatric clinic, "Once it is inside, life has its meaning," and that is just what he meant. Whatever the true answers may look like, they will always depend on the place and the need, or rather necessity, in which the inquirer is found. For a man who has been impotent for years or for a woman who has lived for years without sexual contact, for them Sonneberg's sentence might be the most correct and most important. Later they can consider other questions about the meaning of life.

The answer to the question about the search for meaning, direction and fulfillment will always depend on the degree of suffering and searching of the inquiring mind. In order to see more clearly, we need a spiritual perspective outside of our conscious preoccupation. Even Eros, the "dream," the "unknown," which we often seek and seldom find, lies beyond our mental preoccupation. We always look for it in certain persons or events until we realize that we are not going to find it there. Like Goethe, we restlessly go from one place to another, we sense the nearness of the sought after object, and then suddenly feel the impulse to flee. Our longing for the desired woman keeps us awake at night, and when she is standing or lying before us, we do not know what to do. What we are looking for always appears to be beyond our grasp. Before committing suicide, Heinrich von Kleist wrote, "It is inconsolable and indescribable, my yearning to always seek elsewhere that which I have yet never found in any place." This seemed to be the fate of all the German romanticists – and until today has been the overall human fate as well.

In the longing of the genders for one another, what plays an important role is the hint of approaching lust that we have all secretly anticipated so many times in our fantasies. We men turn our heads around and look at women's bodies because we carry within ourselves a vision of physical intimacy which is hardly ever realized, because we are unable to communicate with each other and because our whole social structure would collapse if we started to follow our sexual visions. It's about sex, but what kind of sex! Lust is the most profound and most beautiful form of exaltation, which encompasses touching, cries of joy, happiness, tears, reticence of the soul and all of the wonderful basic facts of the genders which are irrefutably present as a possibility and as a life goal. This lust is truly the goal of our longing, the meaning of sensuality, the last tear of hidden pain and the first tear of a greater joy. But it demands a different form of existence, one in which it can achieve a continual birth. It demands other social institutions to accommodate our erotic encounters, as well as other spiritual values that will eventually enable us to believe in the happiness, which we already carry within ourselves as a result of our organic composition. It also demands the release from all fixations and inhibitions with which we normally suffocate that little bit of happiness we have just found. Today, however, we can see through the pain that we have inflicted upon ourselves through our false love programs, and can therefore place our hopes in a more solid foundation. This inheritance of pain and hope, passed down from generation to generation, has brought about a new vision of an erotic culture which is focusing on the carnal aspects of love without abandoning its spiritual quality. It is taking place without false intimacy and restrictive relationships, and yet with all the concrete cooperation and responsibility of the individuals participating. An image of a new human being is emerging who has overcome this constraint to see in its face the natural glow of a being who has once again become part of nature, the beauty of that simplicity, of that truth.

Sexuality is popularly called "issue number one." We should not try to hide behind this truth, but rather go a little bit beyond it. What this pearl of wisdom tells us, which everyone knows anyway, even if we do not want to admit it: The subject we think about most, that moves us the most and for which we make the greatest effort, is sexuality. "I would walk a mile for a Camel" is the slogan for the cigarette commercial. "I would go thousands of miles for one single sexual adventure" is the general principle of the tourist industry. People are really just looking for one thing.

But what? What is this one thing? What do they really want from it? Why does it seem to happen so seldom? Why are they so unsatisfied? Why is it that they finally give up this one thing and begin to devote themselves to completely different things? If they want that one thing, which basically everyone wants, why don't they put more care and effort into finding more possibilities for realizing it? And why don't they express their desires more clearly? This must be a strange race. Or is it all a result of their shyness? Are they all so unhappy because of their inhibitions?

Feb 2

I would briefly like to mention a Nizami fairytale about the "Lost Paradise." On his quest to discover all human secrets, an emperor of ancient China goes to a city where all men are dressed in black. They emanate an aura of beauty, strength and mourning. On their search for ultimate bliss, they had all entered the kingdom of the Fairy Queen and her beautiful maidens. As they intimately connect with one woman after another, there is a steadily growing desire within the men to receive absolute fulfillment from the Queen. After thirty nights each man finally succeeds in reaching the Queen. Then it seems as if their desires will be redeemed, but she suddenly disappears. The entrancing image dissolves just like rudely being awakened from a pleasant dream. One can easily relate to the men and their desires, even though it is extremely difficult to capture in words, and it is naive to think that one can achieve this fulfillment with a single person. The consummation of this redeeming lust can no longer come entirely from the outside. We are talking about a way of life which is capable of achieving this absolute fulfillment, and a life, which in fact carries this potential within itself. The story about the lost paradise, written in Persia at the beginning of the 13th century is so moving because it

40

contains a truth which everyone senses immediately, a truth which everyone already knows: that Eros is the source of life and that it is unfulfilled. The piece is moving in the same way as The Sorrows of Young Werther for example, which Goethe wrote as a young man and which all of Europe cried over. After reading the book, Napoleon, who otherwise was not known to be a romantic, thought it absolutely necessary to meet the man capable of writing such verse. What is the story all about? It is about love and especially about the hopelessness of love. Despite Lotte's affection, Werther must commit suicide because he sees no chance of reaching his goal. So what was his goal, and why was his situation so hopeless? Once again we come to the heart of the matter. The goal was – as always in such dramatic love stories – the consummate, sexual and archetypal desire and union with "the woman," not necessarily or specifically with Lotte. The goal could not be attained for two reasons. Firstly because there was no opportunity for Werther of having a direct sexual encounter, and he would not even have known how to handle it anyway. Secondly because there was no place for free love in early German romanticism. The romanticists sought their obscure and arcane happiness in the idealized figure of the one and only woman, whether she is called Maria, Diotima, Helena or Lotte. Werther's adoration and idealization of Lotte was the sign of a forever unsatisfied desire. But how should a woman react to masculine desire when it does not lead to action, to physical consummation?

The conscious or unconscious goal is always the penetration into the "core" by means of sexual union. But if it is "only" that, if the goal is merely of the flesh, why then should it be so unattainable?

There are real yet hidden treasures in the sexual core which we have not been able to tap through the previous channels of love. Or in other words: Because the way in which we have until now sought fulfillment and tried to anchor our happiness did not correspond to the nature of the sought after goal.

A man drives away a woman when he attempts to win her by false methods, and he turns away good fortune when he is too ignorant of it and tries to force it by false methods. The fulfillment of longing requires the initiation into a new process of perception and realization.

The ancient myth of the buried treasure is identical with the myth of hidden sexual fulfillment. That is the real and concrete core of the archetypal symbolism, the true secret of inner tension upon which the myth thrives. Grimm's fairytales do the same. The history of literature from the Gilgamesh epic to Kafka's "castle" has been dominated below the surface by the theme of an unattainable sexual fruit. The sought after treasure is usually found in remote places on Earth – beneath the ocean, on an island, on a precipitous mountain peak or in a dark forest. It is surrounded by demons and nasty guards. Whoever still wants to find it must be prepared to meet one mortal danger after another. The implications of what they say are incredible. There appears to be a mortal danger involved in wanting to reach the treasure, as dangerous as a fire-breathing dragon clutching the maiden in its claws and the hero who wants to free her with poison and fire.

It is always shocking to see how animistic awe, sexual demonism and cultural repression of urges are combined and compressed into such gruesome specters in the mythological human soul. In the course of human history, we have made the fulfillment of our longing more difficult or even impossible through the merciless treatment of those who could not keep their fingers from the desired fruits. After using the most brutal means to burn sexual desire out of the flesh, the church then offered consolation in an imaginary hereafter. Not fulfillment in this world, but redemption in the next world, that has been the spiritual slogan for centuries. We are thus correct in saying that the core of love is not so easy to find under the circumstances which our cultural history has bequeathed upon us. We are still stuck in that same old slave mentality, not in such an extreme and blatant manner as in the past, but more subtly. It proclaims that the inaccessible treasure is a sin and its renunciation is wisdom, suffering is necessary and the tantalizing grapes are sour because they hang too high. **And from the perspective of a man, these grapes still hang on the body of a woman.**

In the face of the existing general structures which dominate the world of sexual love, a culture which advocates complete erotic fulfillment may appear to be a remote and unrealistic utopia, or simply pleasant daydreaming, but in no way a potential reality. This is what we have always thought about love. Something has always kept us from taking control of our own destiny and changing the old structures once and for all by employing our intellect. Today we believe that we are capable of anything, but regarding our concepts about sex and love we still stick to the same old deep-rooted fairytales of our past.

Outside in front of the window the neighbors' boy is playing with his remote control toy car. There is no apparent connection between his hand and the car, and yet it goes along and obeys his will! A true miracle. If we had mentioned that fifty years ago as a concrete technological utopia, they would have considered us to be completely out of our mind. But today, only fifty years later, it is so commonplace that the young boy takes it for granted as he is growing up. Shouldn't we also try to work with a similarly progressive manner of thinking in the area of love that is today so natural in the area of technology?

The buried treasure and the lost paradise are found in no other place but in ourselves. I do not mean every individual, I mean human beings collectively, as a genus, which consists of two genders. The roots of a worthwhile future and a world without fear or violence lie in a new relationship between the genders. This book will gradually make clear what kind of new relationship is meant. Our home here on Earth, our true and final goal, will be present when we have overcome our sexual barriers and no longer feel the need to escape from this world.

arable of the Mount

Our world has become damn inhospitable, and life difficult, but despite all the doomsday tendencies, this age will only be one station on the way to our eternal becoming. The spirit of life goes on. In a time that is so spiritually disoriented as ours, it is only natural that we have lost touch with our spiritual foundations, sources, impulses and limits. Many people go off on their own path, in order to extract from the world that which they were unable to find in their conventional and bourgeois existence. Reinhold Messner had experiences in the death zones of high mountain regions which, if we could take part in them, would bring us further. Rüdiger Nehberg, the great adventurer, took risks upon himself which he was only able to survive because he possessed an unshakable sense of calm and intuition. Domenica, Germany's "last whore," carried out her job to the utmost with such compassionate love, and now, in an unspeakable milieu, practices a form of altruism which a Christian priest could imagine (if he could, it is likely that he would no longer be a priest). Gia Fu Feng, the late Tai Chi master, taught us a contemporary version of Taoism which we will never forget. The Hopi and the Cherokee Indians have preserved a type of natural wisdom which we can no longer do without. We could continue for quite some time. All of these people and groups have made some progress to overcoming and healing the overall problem which confronts us, an inroad to which they have steadfastly remained faithful. But they were and are not connected with one another; often they do not even know anything about one another. Speaking metaphorically, they have all come from various directions and climbed the same mountain without seeing the others who came from different directions. They do not see and recognize one another until they have reached the top.

But will they make it? Do they possess sufficient means to achieve a true communication and human communion together with the others? Where are the wayfarers on the mountain who, step by step, recognize and work on the theme of love between the genders? Have they remained unknown because they got dizzy?

This is the moral of the parable: It is certainly not enough to deal only with the sexual theme. There is more to us than just sexuality, and the truth can never be pinned down to one single path. Although it is generally still beyond public notice, the spiritual and physical pioneers of our time are probing the virgin territory that we will all need in order to reach a greater and more intelligent era. But without the additional work on the sexual issue and without the core work on the unavoidable inner questions, nobody will get to the top. Most of us are unable to pursue such daring escapades of the mind and heart, because they are too dubious and too bizarre, too heroic and too solitary. If we do not nourish them with the warm currents of sensual love, they will always remain too exotic and beyond our reach. The fight for the freeing of love is sort of like conquering the peaks as well. But the goal of the enterprise is to bring happiness down from the mountains and anchor it in the Earth so deeply and firmly that even the valleys begin to blossom. What could be more appropriate for this task than a true understanding between the genders about their most intimate needs and wishes?

From the Bliss of First Love to the Daily Routine of Marriage

Can you imagine that these normal, gray, adult human beings who overpopulate the world once loved? Can you believe that these couples were once in love? Can we imagine our own parents as a glowing, amorous couple? What has occurred within their souls in these few years or decades that has caused them to drift so far away from love? This destiny of lost love has been passed on from one generation to another for centuries. When children are growing up, usually the love between their parents has already died out.

There must be something very potent in relationships which after some time becomes stronger than love and which aims to destroy it at all costs. Neither the most sincere oath of loyalty nor mutual assurances of "till death do us part" will help any more. There is apparently nothing that can be done against the power of creeping mistrust and the onset of boredom. I have never seen any loving relationship anywhere in which the partners were still in love, horny and faithful after 20 years. Or if they were faithful, then only by sacrificing Eros. Or if they still had sex regularly, then without real desire. Or if they stayed with each other despite all the difficulties, then it was for reasons of security and not because of the fire of love.

Because this structural shift from love to daily routine happens everywhere, people apparently accept it as normal. Thirty or forty-year-olds seem to think it is normal that at this age they should be working and no longer loving. It would appear to them absurd to fall in love again, such that they might blush when their eyes met. They sincerely believe that the arousal of the heart and vibration of the body belong exclusively to youth. In a certain way they are right, but only in terms of statistics. Because love in most cases does die at a young age, adults later believe that they have nothing more to do with it. The 68-year-old Emma Goldmann was so aroused by a sexual love experience that all her cells jubilated and she was almost ashamed at having such an experience at this age. But in reality love is not restricted to a particular age, and neither are the beautiful things that accompany love, such as a pounding heart, anticipation, bliss and lust. We human beings have performed an historic miracle with our system of marriage, family and society, whereby the bliss of love in thousands upon thousands of couples was restricted to only the first few days or years and then ultimately extinguished. For someone seeing and thinking clearly, this belongs to the cruelest, most horrible "cultural achievements" of our race.

I would strongly recommend to all those who have just fallen in love to think twice before they get caught in the same trap.

"Blushing he follows her tracks
and is blithesome upon her greeting;
in the meadows he seeks the most beautiful,
with which he adorns his love."

~ Friedrich Schiller

When we are in love in this way, we do not think about loyalty or partnership, about duration or consolidation. We hardly know anything about the person we are in love with. We only have an immense dream and an uncontrollable wish to be together with the object of our desire and to remain so forever. We did not receive a meaningful example of living together from our parents, nor did we receive any knowledge of how to live together in such a way so as to give love permanence. Usually they do not have anything better to do than to take this morsel of happiness and secure it, shield it, isolate it – in short, to attach it to themselves once and for all and, if possible, to etch it in stone forever in the form of a life-long contract, so that the treasure is never lost again. Thus they get married. Bang. Then they rent an apartment and decorate it. Bang. Then they have children. Bang. Then they want to build their own house. Bang!

They ignore the most elementary things and soon the wrangling and bickering will begin. They will treat each other like children, reproach and suspect each other, and keep each other under surveillance. If they are both attractive, they will not tolerate their partner flirting with others. It is silently overlooked that these offers would actually be gladly accepted. They know one another's desire for new contacts because it is the same desire in both of them. They therefore let this subject pass over in silence. But sooner or later the moment arrives when this frail equilibrium of silence collapses and either one or the other begins to explode.

They will say to themselves that they imagined everything to be completely different, that it was the other who broke a promise or did something else just as horrible. They will begin to observe each other intentionally, in order to catch their partner cheating and lying, because both of them know that they do the same thing. This is how the famous vicious cycle of mistrust comes into being, from which there is no escape, assuming the normal conditions of a couple relationship and the general need for social recognition, career, etc. Under such circumstances one generally has no other choice but to abstain from sex and love or to secretly get it elsewhere. In both cases, the relationship has failed. Neither of the two is actually guilty in this strange play. The guilty one is the social stage, the institution of marriage itself, which does not suit the play as long as the play is called love. There is hardly anything else that turns us off more than this stage, and nothing else that turns us on more than the play that is supposed to be acted upon this stage with such burning desire. Performing the dramatic composition called "Love and Desire" on the stage of marriage is just as impossible as performing it on Broadway, where two charlatans try to turn on the audience by presenting an evening show set in a red-light district. Each performance is just as artificial and stale as the other.

My intention here is not to spoil anyone's appetite for love. I am not waging war on couple relationships. They should not be destroyed; they should be saved. But in order to achieve this, the partners must fulfill certain conditions. They have to know that they will not get very far with jealousy and their narrow view of loyalty. Furthermore, love can only be preserved when it is not necessary to isolate it and protect it from the outside; it must be allowed to pursue its natural impulse to expand. In plain English, the partners need a group of friends with whom they can share and relate experiences and where it is possible to speak about all the inevitable difficulties and conflicts in a frank and honest manner. We are certainly demanding too much if we expect two lovers alone to solve all the issues and problems which maltreated Eros has accumulated over the past centuries. That is beyond the capacity of even the best intentions and the keenest intelligence. We have simply done too much to ourselves and our longing in the course of history; we have betrayed love and in its place we have invented a false morality; we have transformed all the once pristine values which were associated with love, Eros, sexuality, friendship and loyalty into petty and trifling matters of a petty and trifling life. It is obvious that sooner or later the moment will arrive where we can no longer talk about anything in a truthful manner. If we did, our entire life of substitutes would collapse; we might lose our job and not have enough money to buy a new car or a house. So instead we prefer to do without truth. But where we avoid truth and confrontation in a relationship, the dullness of daily routine is already preprogrammed. Nothing makes a relationship more exciting than the truth, for that is the only way in which we can begin to discover each other.

In the initial stage of their being in love, the two lovers have no wish to discover each other. They only want to be together, nothing more. They love emotionally, and hope it will stay that way. When they then succeed in sleeping with each other for the first time, they usually have no idea who the other person is lying in bed. Oddly enough, they generally do not truly know each other until they have separated for good. They simply failed to ask beforehand; when it would have been necessary, there was no propitious opportunity to do so because they had already become so fixed in their habits and routines. Everyone who has experienced it, or whose friends have experienced it, knows how this system works. C'est la vie – and it will stay that way if we do not change it. The most important change consists in allowing both partners to pursue sexual fantasies and desires with others without having to give up their love relationship because of it. That is what the next section is about.

Free Love and Couple Relationships

Thus spoke the bee to the exceptionally beautiful flower that he had just found, now you belong to me and you may have no other bees than me.

Thus spoke the shivering man to the sun, which had just begun to warm him, now you belong to me and you may not give your warmth to anybody else.

Thus spoke the wallflower, I love the lilac, but he is loved by so many others, so I will withdraw my love. And the wallflower wilted.

When it comes to love, this is how most people still think. We could continue with a litany of wholly absurd phrases which all have the surprising trait in common that they are actually manifested in the love life of the contemporary human being. In love there seems to be no lower limit when it comes to intelligence and mental sensitivity. We have not agreed on a positive veto where we could say: we will go this far, but not lower. The calculations that we make in life concerning love and sex have nothing at all to do with the matter itself. They are rooted in the mental habits of a society that has always been erotically deprived.

Free love is knowing and healing love. By no means is it opposed to couple relationships, but it is also not fixated on a single partner. One could say that the eyes of the two partners are not constantly directed at each other, but are instead looking with parallel gaze into the world. Here they go on making new contacts, discovering new erotic and spiritual possibilities. Two loving partners, who are joined to each other by knowing love, have absolutely no reason to shut themselves off from this tempting world. The more involved they become in the world, the more they have to communicate to each other and the richer their relationship will be. What bliss it is to meet again in new friendship after such excursions.

It is because of our old ingrained fear that calculations are made in terms of either/or, an arbitrary division which in reality disguises the most beautiful complementarity. In our hearts, many of us have the mentality of a bookkeeper, where calculations are secretly made, where debits and credits are chalked up. They think, for example: "I would like to have this person as my partner, but if we started to practice free love, then I could lose him" – as if we could protect ourselves from this through a couple relationship agreement! Or they love and desire someone, but then think that the other person is already taken and they therefore do not have a chance. Here we have a kind of thinking that contradicts the essence, not only of free love but of any form of love. It seems so self-evident to us that we do not even notice how narrow and false it is. True love does not calculate; it gives freely without thinking about what it gets in return. Free love is also directed at those who are already "taken." Can we really speak of a human being as "taken"? These thoughts stem from petty minds, and those who think them too often develop a petty soul. Free love is the flight of Jonathan Livingston Seagull (from the book by Richard Bach). He too would have liked to settle down with a partner once in a while, if there had been one. Love is a gift that you receive and pass on to others. Sexuality as well is a gift that you enjoy and pass on. If you are constantly calculating when distributing your love energies, as the wallflower did in the above example, then you turn into one. And if you approach love with the mentality of the bee mentioned above, then you soon start buzzing and stinging.

To a large extent free love consists of giving and positive offensive. If you love someone and make if felt, then part of this love is sure to come back to you. The love of a couple relationship should not try to shield itself from free love, because free love is a fact of life and not an arbitrary decision taken by the human being. True partnership needs free love in order for it to grow and remain fresh. It needs free love just as a flower needs water. If water is missing for too long, the flower wilts. If Eros gets too little diversity and not enough new nourishment, then it too will atrophy, even in the best of partnerships. Even if all cultures and nations were to rise up in a cry of protest, the fact remains: Love is free.

Sensual love with all its joy and bliss often begins as fulfilled love in a couple relationship. This love is a natural source for the sexual experience of love and it should therefore be respected and protected. Wherever two serious partners get stuck in their relationship they should be supported, not laconically advised to practice free love. But they should know that there is an alternative for them which could immensely enrich their relationship. Couple love and free love do not contradict each other; they are simply two different stages in the growth process of sensuous love. When love in a couple relationship and free love collide with each other and lead to the well-known hopelessness, then we have made a mistake in our reasoning. It is not a mistake in the abdomen or in the nervous system; it is a mistake in one's thinking. For instance, you are committed to the image of a couple relationship and you meet someone new and think that because of this commitment to the relationship you are not allowed to love or desire someone else. Or conversely, you are committed to free love and suddenly you fall head over heels in love with someone and think that you are not allowed to follow this impulse because it does not conform to your ideas of free love. In both cases you are not following love nor are you following your desire, but a false and artificial thought, an ideology. We tend to make ideologies out of everything that we cannot understand through our own experiences. But sexual love is by nature a principle that invalidates all ideologies. The fact that we are unable to choose between two points of view is reflected by life itself, which in no way forces us to do so. When we do anyway we cannot but lose vitality, truthfulness and our ability to love fully. In love there is no either/or; there is only the expanding power of Eros, the anarchic joy of sensuousness, the flowing fullness and the pleasure of passing it on. In every one of us there is an inner development which leads us to the most varied opinions about sex, depending on what is right for us at the moment. Even though we may swear on couple love today, this does not mean we are betraying anything or being unfaithful in any way by becoming a troubadour of free love a few years later. Discussions and controversies about love in couple relationships and free love are as meaningless as discussions about whether the world is unified or if it is diverse. These kinds of discussions are not normally conducted out of any desire for knowledge, but rather tend to stem from the need for an ideology to safeguard a given situation in life. Ideological judgment has already been spoken before even having an experience and understanding it internally. This ideological principle has been followed by the proponents of both monogamy and free love. Prejudices in love are barriers to knowledge. Love is a basic experience that lies entirely outside of this realm of judgment. Love itself does not constitute a partnership. When it leads to partnership which is no longer sealed off from the outside, that is where a new direction can be found for love between the genders.

To sum up I would like to say a few last words about partnership, which is a highly developed form of relationship between man and woman. It provides us with a model for human relationships that could apply to everybody. It serves the cause of an ever-deepening understanding and connection between the genders as a whole, not just for the two lovers. It is therefore open to all questions of love between the genders and in this way deals with one of the most universal human issues. Partnership and free love do not constitute an opposition; they rather complement and need each other. Sexual climax, falling in love, experiencing sensual delights together are wonderful things, but they do not yet form a partnership. It is a remarkable phenomenon when two people stay together and grow old together, but this does not yet fulfill the conditions for a partnership under the terms outlined here. Two people staying together because they are afraid of being alone is of course is no partnership. A relationship whose self-preservation is dependent on sexual closure toward the outside has not reached the level of a true partnership either. Partnership begins when two people develop a common mental and spiritual basis, which goes beyond mere sexual attraction and succeeds in making communication possible, even when they encounter emotional bad weather. Partnership requires that both partners remain responsible for themselves and that they do not always blame the other. These are two things that are rarely fulfilled in the marriages and relationships of today – the existence of a mental and spiritual basis and self-responsibility of the partners. Until now these things have not fit in with the idea of love nor with the role of women, who have always been allowed to be a bit stupid, as long as they were good looking or good cooks. Partnership has been an almost unattainable goal within the structures of marriage. If you are married, why bother with mental or spiritual understanding? But that is what it is all about today in the era of true emancipation of both genders: man and woman should face each other as partners and truly communicate. Partnership always entails equal rights or, more accurately, equal importance given to both poles. The two can only develop a common partner structure if they are a match for each other and are truly in resonance. A true partnership between an intelligent woman and a stupid man is as unthinkable as a partnership between a lustful woman and a stuffy intellectual bore. It is said that opposites attract, but do they turn each other on as well, and if so, for how long? The fascination of the first contact soon vanishes if their levels are too disparate. Creating a partnership requires knowledge of love from both which protects them from the old traps and which allows them to pull down their fences and let in the outside world. Only then can our dreams prove themselves. The era of partnerships does not lie behind us; it lies ahead of us. It is the era of free love.

The Power of Anonymous Sexuality

There is an erotic difference whether I know a woman well or encounter her as a stranger. What sort of difference is it? If I said to a woman I know very well what I would sexually feel if I were to see her for the first time, I think she would be quite surprised. She would be astonished at the intensity of my desire. She is so familiar with herself that she cannot find anything there especially exciting. She carries the same body every day that she routinely takes care of. She looks at herself in the mirror every day and always sees the same face. Perhaps she knows that she has nice breasts or seductive legs, but that too is part of her daily routine. She is no Marilyn Monroe, after all. She buys nice clothes and even wiggles her hips a little when she walks, since it somehow makes a good impression.

How is her daily self-awareness compatible with the fact that she sexually arouses men she does not know? The same question should be put to the man. He goes about his daily routine and generally does not think about the erotic effect he may have on women (assuming he is not a complete blockhead) simply because he is a man.

What sort of signal is it that can cause such arousal? What signal has this female body sent out that irresistibly draws my attention? How many times have I turned my head around to look without consciously understanding this magic? It is as if the greatest promise, the ultimate fulfillment or the revelation itself were hidden behind the veils. But what promise and what revelation? If I were to tell this to the woman, it would seem to be incredibly silly to her. It would also be awkward because words have very little meaning when the whole organism is conditioned to prevent us from speaking in a rational and frank manner. I know that most men would not even attempt it in such a situation. It would be too exposing and too embarrassing to reveal oneself in that way. Unless he is a cunning macho, whose imposing behavior starts even before he is aroused, then there is no chance of solving such a situation in a sensible manner. Secretly I know that the awakened women experience the same thing, but their chances of starting a sensible initiative are even smaller. We thus see that an unspoken and avoided aspect is present in the daily world of the genders which millions of individuals carry around with them. It is tacitly accepted and internalized until it is forgotten and buried in our everyday routine – and until it inevitably returns.

The difficult aspect of the situation is the following: I do not mean this woman personally, but woman as a generic being, as a member of a class, as the anonymous object of my desire, as an image imprinted on all of my cells and sense organs. I do not react in a deliberate or cautious manner, as a civilized and morally correct human being would do; I react in an unfiltered and spontaneous manner with my entire autonomic nervous system and the fantasy stored within it. I myself usually play the passive role, the role of the victim, even when I only desire to "lay" her. I do not humiliate her; I do not paint an unrealistic picture of her; I am simply under the inescapable influence of a numinous sexual power which she exerts upon me at that moment. At this level there are no words, no opinions, no discussions, and no communication by means of speech. Both sides have the same desire, the same fantasy, and the same power. What is lacking is a non-verbal and non-violent understanding which makes sensitivity and meaningful contact possible despite the sexual arousal. Our culture has unfortunately developed no useful tools to help us in this endeavor. Today we find only mute and passive abstention at this level. We live in a truly erotic culture which knows and even encourages anonymous sexuality for both genders, but which at the same time keeps it beyond our reach.

What would we really do if there were no restrictions on whether or not we were "allowed"? Would we courageously and courteously treat this woman to a drink in a bar and thus lower the non-verbal arousal down to the same level as our familiar and routine existence? It would be nice if we at least did that. But actually…? It's actually about that authentic occurrence which Erica Jong called the "zipless fuck," for which she traveled half way around the world to search for without finding. It's about the one and only, no words, no arrangement, no daily routine. It's not about violence, nor is it about soothing and caressing. It's about the archaic dance of sexuality, about taking and being taken, about surrendering on both sides, about this very particular and unique transcendence of limits. Eros is the power transcending limits; this is where it achieves its fulfillment and recognition. If both partners could do this in an anonymous setting, without lying and nastiness, without fear or violence, then they would emerge from it as exhilarated as they might after experiencing the most profound deja vu. This kind of adventure really does exist, for it has always spurred our most intimate fantasies!

This example shows that sexuality is much more than just a personal encounter between two people. Dorothee Zeemann (in the book Verschwiegene Lust [Silent Lust]) says it is not a love declaration she is looking for, "I want respect in the form of a decent erection, nothing more." Here she expresses in a rather animalistic manner what it is about – sex that transcends the personal and which perhaps arouses us more than anything else. This is equally valid for both men and women. Rooted in the deepest strata of our psyche, sexuality is driven by archetypal energies and strives toward a union which lies beyond all cultural codes. They meet as one man and one woman, nothing more. And when it happens, it is a moment of fulfillment which is not a matter for discussion. When others observe the scene in the bar and notice that the two of them are "doing it," then they themselves become so aroused that they hardly manage to bring the glass to their mouth. Like spiritual energy, pure sexual energy has a cosmic origin. It is one of the true sources of life that leads us across all barriers in a direction that we have not yet dared to probe very deeply, although everyone feels and thinks in this direction. What happens here is not a degradation of our being, but exaltation. We do not go home with a feeling of shame after such an experience, but with a feeling of pride. We "reached" it. We were able to reveal ourselves without being betrayed. In this instant we were not any individual person as defined by society, with a name, age and profession. The special predicates we commonly use to introduce ourselves were unimportant because we only wanted that one thing. In this pure assertion of life, lust and truth, wanting and doing became one.

If we were to raise the objections of the average citizen, we would completely miss the point of the whole thing, because from a rational perspective we were certainly acting irrationally. What distinguishes this experience from others is that we do not examine it and judge it in terms of daily rationality and common sense, which is the source of its releasing and redeeming quality. The rational arguments which are brought against such an encounter are of course only valid under the conditions dictated by society. Under these conditions, such an encounter would hardly ever occur without humiliation or violence. If it did, it would certainly result in even more chaos and confusion afterwards. This example also gives us an idea of what we are missing – those things that society forbids. It also sheds light on the whole complex of issues concerning unlived life and our eternal but unfulfilled longing. Is it possible to create conditions which would enable many people to have such an experience? Is it possible for people to begin using their longing and desire as a basis for thinking through their lives and for deciding on their actions?

Our culture has restricted Eros to the private sphere of two individuals and has thus prevented us from experiencing the deeper zones of sexual magic. But these zones will not let themselves be ignored, as sure as we are human beings. They continue to live underground in secret fantasies; they serve the advertising industry as subconscious seduction; they vibrate in the bodies of whores and saints; they plentifully supply literature with its imagination; they forcefully break out in sexual excesses which are then reported in the press. Society has relegated the explosive power of Eros to the domains of crime and pornography. Today it is this sin which is bringing about the downfall of society, because we are no longer prepared to lead this false existence. It is all too obvious that the numinous powers of Eros no longer fit into society's mold. Too many people drown their secret desire in alcohol; too many people, especially women, have begun to declare war on our sham sexual morality. Sexuality has a two-sided nature – one part of which is socially recognized and the other part of which is repressed; and this is the cause of the disaster that has long plagued humanity. Neither therapy, nor religion, nor fitness, nor a high-fiber diet will help; the only thing that can help is a new guiding force to bring about the liberation of Eros.

The Desire for Surrender, but Without Contempt

The desire to surrender oneself is intrinsic to the sexuality of women and, like everything which is feminine, exists to a smaller extent in men as well. For a woman, love and the longing for self-abandonment are almost identical. It is love that gives sensuality wings. Sexual self-abandonment in an atmosphere of love and trust is heaven on earth.

The yearning for self-abandonment is by no means directed only at one partner, for it is a basic physical and spiritual desire which is a part of human nature, especially feminine nature. The craving for self-abandonment is generally directed towards the man and, consciously or unconsciously, is aroused when a corresponding situation offers itself. This desire appears in many different forms and fantasies, and usually contrasts sharply with what manners and morals prescribe for a respectable woman.

If the young Werther (Goethe) had known what was going on inside his beloved Lotte, if she could have somehow shown it to him, and if he could have somehow given it to her, then the story would surely have ended differently. Feminine desires (and the corresponding masculine ones) clash so severely with society's prejudices and with the woman's own shame that they are generally not shown. But how should one show it in a world where feminine signals sent in this direction can be immediately misunderstood in the most vicious way. The woman wants nothing more and nothing less than to surrender herself, but to whom? And what signals must the man send out so that the woman can be sure that he will not abuse her sexual revelation, which is present in any instance of complete self-abandonment. The feminine desire to be objectified contains very deep elements of submission and subjugation so that the whole issue of misogynous chauvinism and feminist revolt are invoked when this is discussed. But, in the name of knowing love, we must accept sexuality as it is and not as the moral police would like it to be. And thank God it is the way it is. The woman really does want to be made love to, so softly and so firmly that contact is maintained, then she can surrender herself. The fantasies concerning this longing that she carries within herself are substantially cruder and more "Vulgar" than refined taste would permit, but they are correspondingly more genuine. The following is a quote from an article by Beatrice Bartl ("A Women's Manifesto for a New Sexual Humanism"). The article has the title: "The Piece of Meat". I request the readers not to judge too quickly. She writes:

> *"The short moment of the encounter where I am a mere piece of meat ... or a woman on the floor of the blacksmith, who just fucks the piece, simply fucks it. At that moment the man is not this individual but THE man. This is the source of energy for me ... The woman is hit, simply hit, targeted as a woman. And she wants him to understand that and not betray it."*

And she wants him to understand that and not betray it ... and not misuse it sadistically. This is no call to masculine sadism, it is a profound request for cooperation and fairness. The longing to be reduced to a "Piece of meat" contains no desire for masochistic suffering, but a desire for a total impersonal and transpersonal self-abandonment and opening. It's about that wild and archaic sexuality that never allows itself to be integrated into relationships and programs. It lies at the bottom of our soul like a cowering animal that has had to play dead for a very long time, which today is again beginning to raise itself now that it is no longer being thrashed back. These may be harsh images, but they are stored in our unconscious as a result of the historical persecutions of sexuality. It is absolutely necessary that these border regions, where the purest lust comes into contact with masochistic and sadistic tendencies, be integrated into our conscious sexuality. This is the best means to avoid the usual schizophrenia, i.e. the dichotomy between what is taboo and what is accepted.

The text cited here is very direct and perhaps difficult to swallow. But if one has a sensitive and loving blacksmith it could be very promising, and in any case it contains a good and horny bit of reality. I could quote even stronger passages from texts by Sina-

Aline Geissler, Lee Voosen, Heide-Marie Emmermann, and many others. This is a new women's language which seriously discusses one aspect of feminine sexuality. It also addresses something in men which they understand very well, because they too have feminine characteristics. Under the current conditions, however, they can only parry and accept it as anti-women chauvinists, as violent criminals, or not at all. Women have, in addition to all their warmth and caring, a very elementary sexuality which would make us domesticated men tremble if we were to encounter it in full force. Not until a fear-free contact exists between men and women can this greatest of desires be fulfilled without remorse.

When a woman talks about self-abandonment, she also means this type of depersonalization which was alluded to above. This depersonalization has nothing to do with humiliation, but with an archetypal "Materialization" of the female body. In this instant she truly wants to be a sex object for the man, but under the condition that he does not treat her with condemnation and contempt. Lee Voosen writes: "Let me be your material." A certain element of humiliation and apparent violence is in fact found in this feminine desire. But it is not a type of violence that hurts and actually injures; and it is not a type of degradation that in any way elevates the man. Concerning the master and slave games of the sexual trade, it is astonishing how much strength and meaning are generated when both partners remain at the same level without subjugating themselves to each other or elevating themselves above each other. For a woman, degradation sexually means being entirely an object, a body, being taken as an object and being enjoyed as an object. This can bring about more healing than a love affair at times. It means liberation from the psyche and liberation from schmaltz. A woman who is made love to by an intelligent and sensitive man will always stay beautiful. Liz Taylor looked so beautiful and healthy at 58 because her trucker made love to her so well and because she could trust him completely. I would like to know what Alice Schwarzer would have thought about this so-called "Penetration" if she had experienced the same trust.

Feminine sexuality of course does not only consist of self-abandonment. The sexual spectrum of women contains, with different priorities, pretty much the same variations as that of men. The woman as well, when she lets her instincts take over, can become tremendously active. A woman as well can enjoy working on a man sexually until he "Comes". No value judgment should be made here. But this chapter of the book is dedicated to the subject of self-abandonment. In terms of sexual polarity, this is where the deeper feminine core is found, and usually the deeper longing and the deeper shame as well. It is marvelous when a woman says to a man: "I want you". But doesn't she want him sometimes just to be able to "Belong" to him for a period of time? She has him then too, but in a different way.

When aroused in this manner, feminine desire often leads to enslavement. A man who is capable of arousing and satisfying this desire does not need to possess any special aesthetic or moral qualities. Feminine desire is so strong that it takes for granted much that is vulgar, mean, and rude, or even wants it. Herein lies the danger for the woman and for this type of feminine sexuality. What man is able to quench feminine desire without meanness and contempt? Among the existing societal and mental structures there is in fact hardly any opportunity for women to show their anonymous desire and to have it fulfilled in an open and decent manner. This is the reason why women usually begin to abstain from sex after a time. What remains is an unconscious feeling of resentment, a need to revenge the man because he was incapable of copulating with her properly. This latent revenge takes many forms, as for example the motherly governess, who revenges the man by means of an overdose of care and kindness. In a world where feminine sexuality is barely satisfied by men, if at all, every warm-blooded female body is a true system of despair.

As Sina-Aline Geissler, a German author, writes, this despair exists on both sides:

"I wanted to fight in order to be defeated ... I was a power-woman and longed to be tamed. I despised all these men who blushed in

my presence because they were amazed or insecure. Men fell into
great astonishment, then felt inferior, got complexes and hang-ups,
and in the end I had to be their mother to build them up again and
console them, which was contrary to my true nature ..."

And the men who meet such a woman really do get frightened.
They would like to do it, but they are unable. Nobody should pass
a judgment here. It's not just because the are wimps, it has been
a whole history of pain and fear, a history of misunderstanding
and mutual injury, so that it is not so easy for us to forget it. This
desire must be linked with a new knowledge and a new means of
communication on both sides. Otherwise things will continue the
way they are: for one successful experience we find one hundred
which are frustrating. The embarrassing thing for men is not
only that they would have to give up their piggish and predatory
energies, but that they would not know how to act if such behavior
were allowed.

Under the existing societal conditions, women are generally
inhibited in their actions because of their shame. They think they
must have something abnormal and perverse about them because
they crave this type of pure sex again and again. The hidden misery
on both sides will not end until women are permitted to show
their desire for self-abandonment without having to fear contempt
from men, and until men are capable of responding to this feminine
desire without fear or mean thoughts. In order to bring this about,
I think that new places for sexual encounters should be created,
which will be suggested at the end of this book.

Healthy Nymphomania and the Hunger c. Cells

Jesus experienced the reality of the Holy Spirit. He remained "obsessed" by this experience his whole life. Can we therefore say that he had a deviant or abnormal disposition? Van Gogh discovered the sun. He was obsessed with light and color his whole life. Was he "abnormal"? There are people who have discovered sex (this can be a discovery, too). They are obsessed with sex. Does this make them "abnormal"? When it concerns men, it is generally tolerated. When it concerns women, we call it "nymphomania."

Nymphomania represents female sexuality breaking through all the barriers of morality and pretense. The suffering that results from nymphomania is due to the fact that, under the existing conditions, society provides no fulfillment for this breakthrough. A woman under such circumstances feels quite strange, since most other women do not appear to be affected by this drive. One gradually begins to consider oneself abnormal. But "abnormality" is in this case only a statistical concept; it simply means that one's sexual fantasies and desires do not agree with those of the majority of one's contemporaries. It has no pathological significance beyond that. The question as to who is more abnormal in the pathological sense, the majority or the minority, is an issue we will disregard here.

In order to deal with nymphomania in a purposeful way, there is one problem which must be taken into consideration. Sometimes the built-up desire is so overpowering that it is no longer possible to establish any meaningful contact. When this necessity has conditions attached to it, it is very difficult for the man to accommodate the sexual desires of the woman in a good and horny manner. This is not only true for nymphomania, it applies to any situation where a certain need within us has get the upper hand to such an extent that we are no longer able to think of anything else. The more we are fixated on this need, the less it is fulfilled in life. This is true for all those who concentrate their energies too much in search of any one thing, be it in their search for sex, for a life partner or for religious truth. When the search is too one-sided and too intense, the possibility of fulfillment is driven away. It can even lead to a vicious cycle of frustration and inner rage which reaches pathological dimensions. All of us have been inflicted with such anguish from time to time. First of all, it is necessary to have some peace of mind before an alternative means can be found to satisfy or mitigate this excessive hunger. We also need an inner assembly point outside of our needs in order to try it again from a more favorable position.

In the life of a human being it often takes quite a long time for the sexual energies, which arise from the subterranean rumbling of the cells, to pass through all the inner labyrinths and reach the light of day in the form of a pure and undisguised natural power. But once this process has begun and the inner crusts and barriers are broken, the sexual energy that is released is tantamount to a volcanic eruption. The whole organism adapts itself within a very short time and completely concentrates itself on this focal point. It is as if the dormant hunger of years and decades were awakened all at once. The body and soul of the organism have an infinite amount to catch up on. It is natural under such circumstances that the organism should temporarily lose its balance. Those who have been seized in this way by the elemental forces of life can by no means keep their normal balance. This is why a woman who is in such a situation needs human support. Not in the form of hypocritical lecturing, but through the possibility of sexual contacts without fear and shame. If there were only enough men who could accept this offer in a decent way!

Nymphomania is not sexual perversion; it is in principle the neutralization and cancellation of all perversions, because it brings sexual energy to the surface in its purest, most spontaneous and least disguised form. If people knew more about this process and, above all, if they knew more about themselves, then they would also know that the same thing could occur on a different plane of their existence. If all of us were allowed to develop our sexual energy in a free and unobstructed manner, then we would all pass through this stage of infinite sexual hunger at one time or another. We would suffer as well, assuming we have not developed better possibilities for fulfillment by then. If, in the conflict between desire and shame, millions of people were able to choose desire, then the "nymphomaniacs" could suddenly find themselves in the majority and no longer in the minority.

In the clash between desire and shame, there are many reasons for a woman to choose shame, for she senses that the hunger which lies concealed within her desire cannot be quenched very easily. Where can you find someone who is capable of quenching female desire? This question is meant seriously and has nothing to do with contempt of women. The priests and religious spokesmen of our culture have always viewed women as "evil" and "sinful" since they represent the carnal elements – desire and seduction. This has always justified the severe measures that have been taken against women in the course of history, and not just in the witch-hunts of the Middle Ages. Instinctively men have sensed and feared the superior strength of female sexuality.

It will take quite some time before the female gender can recover from the long history of persecution it has been subjected to. The "memories" are engraved in the deepest layers of the soul. Today, when a woman can no longer suppress her own nature and decides in favor of her sexual desires, she is unconsciously confronted with the whole patriarchal history of sexual persecution. If she goes on the offensive by calling her own drive "abnormal" and even seeks medical attention for it, then it may be viewed as a subconscious request for absolution and forgiveness. She has calmed her conscience by doing so, but not her desire.

Nymphomaniacs have had the misfortune of living at the wrong time. Although it appears to them that their own feelings and those of "normal" women are worlds apart, in reality there is no difference in the inner structure; there is only a difference in the degree of sexual manifestation. It is simply "more pronounced" in nymphomaniacs. But that which is present in them exists in others as well, at least structurally, since sexual energy is present everywhere where there are human beings. Just invent an infrared camera that can secretly record people's thoughts and fantasies – strolling through the city for example or shopping in the supermarket or during the halftime break at a football game or at a book fair. If we could see all the sexual thoughts that flash through people's minds – usually for only a few seconds before they are repressed once again – we would find ourselves in a sexual inferno that by far surpasses even our boldest imagination. What should we call this phenomenon of repressed nymphomania? It is much more than this. The human world is so different from what it appears to be that sometimes you wish the whole circus would just vanish and leave behind one big halcyon grin.

The so-called nymphomaniac belongs to that rare type of woman who can no longer say "no" to her unrelenting feminine desire. But, due to the excess pressure and the unfavorable social prerequisites, she has not yet been able to find her own sovereign and convincing "yes." Her condition is symptomatic of the illness of our time, only that she has reached a more advanced stage. In any case, I completely support her desire for sexual fulfillment and would like to help create opportunities for her to achieve this with less difficulty and restraint.

The Compulsion to Lie

"If all the surgeons, all the analysts, all the medicos
could be withdrawn from their activity and gathered
together for a spell in the great bowl at Epidaurus,
if they could discuss in peace and quiet the immediate,
drastic need of humanity at large,
the answer would be forthcoming speedily,
and it would be unanimous:
REVOLUTION.
A worldwide revolution from top to bottom,
in every country, in every class,
in every realm of consciousness."
    ~ Henry Miller, The Colossus of Maroussi

In no other area of life are we driven to lie so much as in the realm of sexuality. The urge is ingrained in us from childhood. Nowhere else has untruth become so deep-rooted and firmly fixed in our nature as it has here. That is why it is so difficult to overcome. It is as if everyone were participating in a conspiracy against the truth. When someone that refuses to take part in the conspiracy is found, then the others have their scapegoat, the victim they seem to need in order to feel safe and protected within the confinement of their perverted morality. It's always the same. Not long ago I read an article in a magazine about female schoolteachers who supposedly sexually abused their pupils. The teachers were between the ages of 28 and 45, the pupils between the ages of 13 and 17. A good and exciting age for both sides. What boy wouldn't like, if he were allowed, to have an exciting meeting with one of his teachers? There is nothing more fantastic and exciting that could happen to him than that. And let's assume that she goes about it in a thoughtful and considerate way, since she too feels desire. What better way is there for an adolescent boy to be sexually initiated? If it were possible to talk about such an erotic encounter, not in terms of dirty jokes and vague hints, but openly and honestly, the boy could be spared so much confusion and suffering in his further sexual development.

And vice-versa – what teacher wouldn't like, if she were allowed, to have an exciting meeting with one of her students? She would not be a warm-blooded woman if the thought did not at least occasionally cross her mind. Just imagine that such thoughts did not have to be immediately repressed, but that it was possible to reflect on them in peace. Just imagine that they could be discussed openly between friends, since they were anyway generally accepted. Just imagine that such a teacher took delight in toying with the idea, would she be wrong in doing so?

She would come to the plain and obvious conclusion that she likes boys who have not yet had a woman. Every woman desires that in one form or another. To be his first woman, to let him come into her, his lustful innocence, his arousal, his clumsiness, his strength. There is no doubt that this is beautiful. Why should there be anything wrong or perverted about it?

It is not the action that is bad, but rather the social conditions in which it takes place, which tend to degrade such actions. In this context it is not uncommon, for example, for one of them to blackmail the other, or something similar. The bad thing about it is that the action cannot occur under conditions of freedom and human decency, because a nosy, sex-crazed, hypocritical mob stares and goggles at everything that spurs its pornographic imagination. In the end, the fear of being discovered is stronger than the friendship that could have resulted from the encounter. And when it is finally revealed, the two in question are forced to blame each other because they perceive this as the only way out of the predicament. Under these circumstances hatred is generated, where love might otherwise have been possible.

It is a never-ending tragedy, but it is the fate of many sexual encounters which transgress the bounds of "normality." The clear losers under these conditions are love and truth, which simply fall by the wayside. People who see themselves forced to perform their social functions because they have no other choice are the same ones who are forced to lie, and they must be certain that nobody notices. In this way they are driven into a warped and perverted double existence, to which their true thoughts, desires, wishes and sometimes even actions are confined. This is because Mr. Clean is always pointing his accusing finger and using the weight of his "healthy" common sense and reason, his public opinion, his strict morality, his unstained vest. This division of existence into that which is shown and that which is hidden is present in all social classes, professions and levels of education. Double moral standards and false pretenses are some of the fundamental principles of our culture. The more morally strict someone behaves outwardly, as for example judges, priests and teachers, the more depraved and degenerate they become internally. Their robes and honors of office protect them from exposure. All youth should know that the moral authorities that confront them are generally worse than they themselves. So much pretense and distortion is not even possible when you're only 15.

It has been said many times, but perhaps it should be said once again: Our false sexual morality is the cause of so many acts of desperation and cruelty. It has not prevented harm and suffering, but has given rise to it. It has not humanized the world; it has terrorized it. It has not filled people with love, but with hatred and fear. It has not helped the misfortunate, but has condemned them. It has attacked lovers of all ages with fire and swords, with inquisition and slander. It has threatened, defiled, impaled, degraded and exterminated in order to free the world of love. It has created churches and dignitaries to sanctify the lie. Finally, it has built hospitals to treat the psychosomatic effects of the destruction it has wrought.

Morality and lying have always been very closely linked, for centuries they have been siblings, and it is taken for granted to such an extent that nobody even cares to think about it anymore. Those who see the connection usually turn cynical or silently resign. Active lovers, however, are not prepared to accept either. Their love only has a chance in the long run if they devote their lives to finishing off this putrid magic.

There is no sense in expressing ideas just because they are "in" at the time. The slogans which profess a free lifestyle in the West are simply ridiculous and absurd, especially if you consider how many people are spiritually devastated and isolated. We have wasted too much time conforming ourselves to the rules of this circus; too much truth and too much potential love have been irrevocably lost. Now it's up to all seekers and lovers to trust their own intuition and find out what is really true and then speak it, since that which is true for oneself is usually true for others as well. What is universally true is that human beings seek greater sexual fulfillment. Once we are in the position to communicate this in a truthful way and act accordingly, Eros will possess the embryonic power to burst out of its asphalt shell. It's within our reach.

False Morality and True Ethics

When false morality is discussed in this book, it doesn't mean that morals are always false. One should not deliberately attempt to lead an amoral life; this would only be the other side of the coin. True conscience is one of the most noble and exalted facilities of the human mind and under all circumstances should be rediscovered, cultivated and obeyed. But our conscience speaks a completely different language than conventional morality. Morals in the old sense are rooted in fear of punishment. True ethics, which are rooted in human conscience, are responsibility, involvement and support for life, all of its embryonic forces and the forces of growth and love. The old morals were nourished on fear; genuine ethical principles are nourished on truth and trust. Only if there is truth and trust can we overcome the old fear-based morals and go on to experience that more profound love which makes us compassionate and ethical creatures. The immorality of traditional culture can only be overcome if we begin to lead a different life among one another. This has a lot to do with truth in love, which is not easy to bring about under the conventional conditions of marriage, couple relationships and jealousy. No one can remain faithful to someone else for 30 years in the traditional sense without at least "deceiving" their partner in their fantasies. Truth in love, ethics in sexuality and long term caring and curiosity for another person are only possible if new forms of coexistence between the genders can be found – these forms must be more open, but not less binding.

What we've learned to call morality today is not, because of the ever-present tendency to hide, twist and reinterpret the truth until it becomes it's opposite. So the existing morality is just the official form of something which has become truly immoral. Our sexual morality has been a major source of all immoral acts. As it has hindered the development of a natural sensuality and enjoyment of life, it has also blocked the genesis of a natural code of ethics. It is not the so-called sins of the flesh that are immoral; it is rather those who have named them so. It is not the so-called original sin that is evil; it is those who have named it original sin that are evil. It is not adultery which is immoral, but rather the seventh commandment which forbids it. It is not the sinful flesh that is weak, but the human mind, which the church and the false prophets have robbed of its courage to search for the truth. If there is an absolute necessity for a re-evaluation of all values anywhere, it is here – but not simply in the sense of negation and reversal. New values do not arise by turning around the old ones; in fact they do not originate from the old ones at all. They arise as a result of a new, stable and long-lasting experience of love, truth and trust.

True ethics grow out of love and joy of existence. Human nature has created us to be good to that which we love, gentle to that which is young and delicate, caring for that which is beautiful. We have sympathy for those who suffer; we truly pity without false sentimentality. In our world of suffering, sympathy is a basic sensation of every moral human being. Here we differ considerably from Nietzsche, who viewed sympathy as a weakness. Like many other heroic men, he simply attempted to overcome his soft heart through harsh mental training, until he himself was finally overcome on that fateful morning in Turin in 1889 when he witnessed a man senselessly beating a horse. The philosopher of the "Ubermensch" then ran over to the horse, laid his arms around its neck and collapsed in tears. Those who understand creation, those who are aware of it and know it, understand this spontaneous act of compassion, an act which has nothing to do with morality. Care and assistance, which occur automatically as a result of perception and feeling, have nothing to do with moral duty; they are spontaneous acts of natural ethics.

The more mature true ethics become, the more closely it is linked to consciousness and reason. After a time it will not only react positively to that which one loves, it will also react differently to that which one dislikes. I do not want to give another version of the Sermon of the Mount, nor do I want to reproduce the lofty Manichean Ethic ("love what is evil"). But genuine ethics, which draw their power from love, trust and truth, are valid for all human beings, even for those who live without these sources and who therefore do evil things. The more closely we are linked to the ethical source of a "knowing love," a love which trusts and understands, and the more we are connected to the morals that come from this type of love, the less we will be able to hate these people. Once we have grasped the connections between disturbed childhood and the later appearance of violence and deception, when we have understood the connections which Alice Miller describes in her books on the psychology of childhood suppression of feelings and emotions, then we can no longer simply abandon ourselves to our instincts of hatred and revenge. This is not to say that we should simply give ourselves over to our enemies and just pray for our evil brothers, but we will adopt a humane and spiritual discipline which no longer consists of an indoctrinated moral code, but instead arises out of our own recognition and experience.

In the spirit of authentic ethics and compassion, we shall call all things ethical which promote the elementary forces of growth – warmth, love and understanding. Always arising from living contact and experience, "ethical" refers to the courageous and unsentimental cooperation with nature and the rest of creation instead of controlling and exploiting it. An ethical human being would not wear a fur coat for whose production animals were murdered in fur farms or by trapping.

Suppressed Longing and Unlived Life

"You don't regret the sins you committed,
you regret the ones you failed to commit."

~ An elder woman from Verschwiegene Lust [Silent Lust]

Our sex lives have always been much more active in our fantasies than in reality. What are all our words compared to that which we dare not say! What are our visible lives compared to those parts which we hide! What are ten marital sex acts compared to one honest and juicy masturbation fantasy! Are we aware of the fact that we have never gone public with this core aspect of our lives, that we have never entered into real relationships with real human beings, that this core aspect of us has never seen the light of the day? When will we come to realize that proper, lawful sex often takes on the function of suppressing the sex that truly excites us, that we dream about? Why do we do this?

When we asked our parents if they were satisfied with their lives, they said yes because they didn't know anything else. When I ask a married woman if she is satisfied with her love life, she says yes as well because she hardly has any opportunity to choose a different one from the one she leads. There is no use asking such questions as long as there are no means of comparison and as long as there is no possibility of change anyway. Under such circumstances it may in fact be a bad idea to consider the truth too closely, since it hurts even more when you realize there is no way out. In my first semester of psychology we had to fill out a wonderful questionnaire. One of the questions was, "Are you satisfied with your sex life?" As I had none whatsoever, I answered yes. I'm not even sure if I was lying or telling the truth.

I only know that we are not satisfied with our lives. I was always happy when I heard or read anything that clearly stated this opinion without exaggerating or being dramatic about it. This book makes no attempt to stage a powerful drama, no matter how effective it may be. It is concerned with finding ways to motivate us to assess our situation and act accordingly. Proof of the sobering balance is for me the fate of the Swiss teacher and writer Fritz Zorn, who got cancer when he was 30 years old and thus had no time in his remaining two years of life for sentimentalities and half-truths. While confronting his approaching death, he wrote the book Mars (see bibliography), in which he portrayed his sexual agony in a straightforward, sober and intelligent way. We no longer have him, since he died after writing the book, but we have the book. It is a document of our times. If we were to admit this unfortunate state of affairs, we would probably talk less nonsense and more truth, and even view the world a bit more clearly. There would be no reason for depression or despair if we could decide to begin to be honest about this. Except for those who conceal their feelings and isolate themselves, there is no need to give up hope.

The fresh and encouraging thing about Fritz Zorn, despite his early death, is the positive "no" which he writes across his life. There is certainly a positive "yes" as well. There is a justifiable philosophy of saying "yes," as long as one experiences saying "no" in a radical way to all the ways we betray ourselves. I always recommend saving that final "yes" for the last ten years of life after having devoted oneself to the big "no" in all its beauty and truth, having refused to accept anything other than what we want. When I look at it closely, what is so great about life that really makes it worth loving? Who or what has been important enough to me to warrant complete commitment? What inner and complete conviction have I been able to gain from life, to which I would be willing to devote all my energies, unconditionally, with no ifs, ands, or buts?

In blossoming sentimentality under blossoming cherry trees on blossoming meadows, I used to have strange, unquenchable yearnings. I had dreams and lust and callings, year after year. Are they gone now? I used to be afraid when confronted by certain special girls. Is that over now? At 15 I hardly knew anything, now that I'm almost 50 I know quite a bit more, but have I come closer to that which was for me the goal and meaning of life? Every effort, every bit of self-punishment and every injustice against others has carved a new wrinkle into my face, but am I really sure that this struggle has been worthwhile? I still stand on the spring meadows full of longing; I still have the same prickling sensation when I see women; I still have the same dream of a life without fear and without chicken-hearted compromises. Life is not even close to being over, not at 50 and not at 80, but it has never really been lived either. In a way, it has all been a preparation.

If I were a woman, it would certainly have been more difficult. Somewhere along the way I would have lost my overall perspective. After having accrued a certain amount of wrinkles and other physical defects, I would have come to the conclusion that I had grown too old and too worn out for a promising sex life. Women generally begin to think along these lines when they are as young as 30. This is where the assumption or even the certainty begins that life has passed you by. One should reflect on this for just a moment. People who are actually at the height of their creative potential begin to have the feeling that they have missed out on life, that they have made too many mistakes and not found what they were looking for. They suffer from pangs of remorse and desire, not in any constructive way, but in a way that only leads to defeat and resignation, as they see no other way out. They may occasionally make a comeback or two, but eventually they resort to other means in order to get through the remaining decades more or less unscathed.

After the shine and the glory are gone, emptiness sometimes sets in. There is usually very little left of the fame that we have achieved in life. What will happen to the world champion boxer Mike Tyson when his money is spent? What happened to the tennis champion Björn Borg when he stopped playing tennis? How long are we going to let ourselves be deceived by temporary success and suppress the real issues? I have always liked Boris Becker. Despite all of society's temptations, he has succeeded in placing the issues of life higher than his tennis scores. He will certainly not be left standing with empty hands when his tennis career is over. Supported by those who love him, he will remain in contact with life and not let himself be corrupted by advertising offers from Adidas, which they have not yet attempted, because they noticed that he is a human being and not a puppet.

I have drifted away from the subject a bit so as to avoid beginning the discussion straight off with sex. But in the end, unlived life always consists of unlived love and unlived sexuality, a point which has already been made. I would however like to again mention the book "Verschwiegene Lust" [Silent Lust], in which women over 60 talk about their sexual love life. They are at an age where life is considered "over," and yet claim that they are in the middle of everything – in the middle of their sexual desires and the issues of love, Eros and friendship. They are much more honest than others, because they don't have anything to lose. What would happen if everyone spoke like that, before they reach the age of 60 or 80? What would happen if their dreamy youth were to undergo a good, solid change of course so that they could stop missing out on all the important things in life?

Over 30% of the population in Hamburg is made up of men and women that live alone. There are masses of concrete blocks consisting of apartments for so-called "singles." These singles are usually over 30 and often over 40. In this case, the misery of unlived life has been reproduced in the very architecture that surrounds us. I would not like to be in their place. But neither do I want to emphasize the hopelessness of their lives, which they themselves already believe in. If the discos are no longer an alternative, then perhaps there are other possibilities for contact and zest for life. This book might even be passed around in such cases. It would at least be a starting point. Someday it will certainly be possible to transform this whole singles' existence and supply it with a new perspective. These people don't just need new contacts; it is above all desire and courage that they need for rebuilding their lives. For every single, whether man or woman, there are numerous possibilities of finding a way out of this despairing situation – if he or she is prepared to take the risks.

To conclude, so no one thinks that singles have gotten the worst of the deal in our society… It is often even more hopeless in the so-called love relationships and marriages. When for example married couples sit in front of the television in the evening in the most cozy state of loneliness and emptiness, and watch everything they missed out on in life on the TV screen … When each one secretly thinks of something the other is thinking which they are not allowed to say openly … When the "cultivated" part of humanity, the white race in Europe and North America, lets itself be fooled in this way and does nothing about it … The hoodlums of course comment on all this insanity in their own way. They use violence to get their share of adventure in life, which they are unable to achieve in a more peaceful way.

As a result of its disastrous cultural tradition, our social existence has developed two separate levels: the first consisting of our inner, hidden, burning desires and fantasies, the second consisting of the stage where we appear as normal, respectable citizens. Many people have gone berserk as a result of this type of schizophrenia. As long as the two levels remain separated, people will be under the spell of that mysterious disease called "Unlived Life."

Last Night in the Bar

This story takes place at a relatively prominent locale in Frankfurt. I know the couple that runs the bar. Both are attractive, in their early thirties, affluent and yet unfulfilled. They have not completely given up their longing for something different. But now what? Concerning this question, they have made a contract of sorts – they have simply agreed not to talk about it. She meets secretly with … He meets secretly with … They suspect or even know it, but they are "fair" and never mention it. And the waitresses: two women with voluptuous breasts. It is a detail which is impossible to overlook. When he looks at them he begins to have certain thoughts. But when he feels that she notices these thoughts, he pretends to be very businesslike and suddenly acts as if he were not thinking about anything. A seemingly effective method of covering up their secret, this type of jumping action has become so common that the whole thing looks like one big business adventure. Then suddenly her ex-boyfriend from Yugoslavia appears on the scene. He has in fact come because of her, but she has to take care of business behind the counter. She would love to make a rendezvous with him, but that could cause serious problems with her husband. So just forget it. Then an 18-year-old comes in who is interested in the older of the two waitresses, because she is so feminine, motherly and earthy, but she has to serve the other customers. And what customers they are! They're hardly able to conceal their voyeuristic appetites behind the menus and wine bottles.

And everything happens without one word being spoken about it. It is a good example of the preceding chapter about how our society consists of two levels. I would have gladly whispered something into her ear, but what, seeing how she is caught up in this system. The two restaurant owners are in the process of making a decision: money or love, business or truth, social rank or vitality in life? It appears that they have already made their decision. They are still just as nice to be with as before, but they have become part of something else. They wanted to set up an alternative bar. Now they're in the money and they go on vacation to the Caribbean. I'll just order another small glass of beer and think about it once more. Who staged all this, and why do they take part?

My Friend Martin

Martin is conspicuous, in his mid-forties, a gifted architect and tirelessly active as a philosopher and artist. He recently saw his girlfriend again after a long period of separation. He picked her up at the train station and announced that he wished to be together with her again on a steady basis. Her reaction was reserved and rather cool. Internally, Martin reacted immediately, but outwardly he has the ability to give the impression of a Zen master, even if his emotions are going berserk. They drove together through a town on Lake Constance in southern Germany and came upon a railroad crossing with the gates down. Martin stepped on the gas and swerved through the gates, the train missing him by only a few feet. Others have not been so lucky.

It was a symbolic gesture. The gate, which internally cannot be overcome, is broken through externally in ecstatic determination. This often happens to men when they fail to reach their feminine destination. They don't get the girl they want and start committing acts of heroism. They live in a symbolic world where that which they really search and long for remains out of reach, over and again, and which must then be achieved in the form of a symbolic action. For this, no peak is too high, no desert is too vast, no racetrack is too dangerous; the man simply goes for broke. He doesn't cling to the woman in a soft and connected way; he does what his nature dictates; he drives the bolts of his mind into the substance of the world. He tends to express himself symbolically because he is unable to get what he really wants. So in this way he has become a philosopher replacing the experiences he desires with theories or symbols. He has practiced this for centuries, and has had no choice, since he has been separated from women for too long.

We all more or less lead a symbolic life, from our car to the brand of cigarettes we smoke. This remains so as long as we have not yet come together, the man with the woman and the woman with the man, the two genders merged. It is our permanent life of not being able to have what we want that drives us to such symbolic actions. It is a birth process, and all these dramatic excesses take us toward it. What will or wants to be born? It is always love; it is always this innermost spiritual and sensual home of the genders. It is never anything else; it only appears in alternative forms as long as its true realization is still obstructed. Thus heroism and contempt of death are manifested, where in fact love was intended. Hardness is displayed where softness was meant. Men show violence at moments when they would actually like to surrender themselves. We live in a symbolic world of reversed values.

Martin has a marked sensual propensity, I have seen him cook many times and have been delighted. But as a symbolist and philosopher he is so hooked on the mind that he must examine and question all sensual aspects of life before experiencing them firsthand. I suspect that he spent many previous lives in monastic schools in order to free his being from that area below his belt. Today he is as aloof and sexy as creaking wood. But he cooks and dances like a satyr. Orality and sexuality, mouth and genitals, pleasure through food and pleasure through sex, they all belong together in the divine composition of our bodies. If Martin learns to make love as well as he can cook, he'll never have to break through a railroad crossing again.

Sexuality between Longing and Shame

Has anyone ever read the book Fear of Flying by Erica Jong and really absorbed it without commenting on it first? Her longing for the "zipless fuck" is the conscious or unconscious longing of every human body. Has anyone ever read Anais Nin's Delta of Venus without having to assure oneself that it is only literature? She herself was so embarrassed about her confessions that she claimed that she had only written it for money. Has anyone ever read such books without being gripped in one's innermost cells by their candid truthfulness? Has anyone ever read Bukowski or Henry Miller without getting genuinely and sincerely horny? What is being described in these books is genuine Eros. The further it is removed from real life, the more strongly it inspires and stimulates our fantasies. They are books that affirm sexuality, and the emotions within us to which they appeal are positive ones. An intense and boundless longing burns within us after such an experience, a heaven and hell of unlived possibilities. And they are all inside of that decent body, covered by those decent clothes, underclothes and ties, topped off by that decent face with a smug expression of decent apathy. We're so clever. If the art of camouflage of some marine creatures or of the chameleon has reached an astonishing level of perfection, it is nothing compared to the mimicry achieved by human beings. A warm body is seething with desire and bursting at the seams, and it is wearing glasses and reading a newspaper. A secretary is doing her mandatory typing and close at hand she keeps her vibrator in her purse. An attractive man makes an attractive woman a very enticing offer, but out of pure desire she says no. A preacher seduces his underage niece and yet from the pulpit he rants and raves against fornication. Human beings are the most amazing animals in the zoo of evolution because we apply our camouflage not to our advantage, but to our disadvantage.

The shame goes as deep as the desire. There is a book by Anja Meulenbelt called Shame is Over. It serves as a good eye-opener or impetus for further thought, but in reality shame is not close to being over. Instead, it has only just begun to make us aware of its full extent. I am not talking about natural shame, which probably affects everyone upon the awakening of his or her first sexual desires. These initial steps are always tender and fragile. A stirring, a bit of shame, chastity and shyness are part of every erotic encounter, not just during youth. Shame tenses the inner strings of the delicate music of our feelings and sets the right pace for two people to come together. But it is also receptive to the most beautiful shamelessness, if the situation is ripe for it. But I am talking about the other type of shame, which hinders this openness. It does not arise naturally from the situation, but rather from the fear of disapproving glances and thoughts of others. This shame is the true obstacle, which causes most of us to fail even if we attempt to force ourselves to be free.

The shame of what others might think about us and the equally deep-rooted shame of our self-image, which is not compatible with the vulnerability and contortions of sexuality, are not part of our sexuality; they are part of our culture. The spiritual and political authorities and dignitaries of this culture have always had to pay close attention to labels and outward appearances in order to avoid exposing their filth and indecency. Imagine a child peeping through the doorway and listening to her strict aunt's screams of ecstatic pleasure. Or a pupil at school who secretly hears his teacher moaning and groaning in the restroom. Once we have seen our role models in such scandalous positions, we no longer believe in their wisdom and all-pervading power. A society based on authority and oppression, instead of life and truth, is compelled to do everything possible to avoid such embarrassments. This in turn induces us, even as children, to develop a picture of human beings and their dignity, which is not at all consistent with our experience of sexuality.

Wilhelm Reich called the sexual revolution the second Copernican revolution. In the first revolution, we lost our anthropocentric pride when we discovered that our little planet and we were not the focal point of the universe. In the second revolution, we lose our traditional dignity when we are forced to accept facts that contradict this dignity. The same men and women who strut around in public with a tie and dry cleaned trousers, with a suit and a proud gait, perform the throbbing, pumping movements of a jellyfish as they thrash about in bed at night. The same people who otherwise speak in well-chosen phrases now make the basic sounds of the flesh. The metamorphosis could hardly be more striking. And the positions, the secretly desired motions and gestures, the instinctive tendency toward the most total, spread out and shameless opening! Nietzsche, the mighty revolutionary of the spirit, would have blushed at the mere thought of such fornication. And just think about our mothers! They sensed the sweet delights of this "disgraceful act." All the more reason for them to reject and condemn it. The essence of shame is connected with the essence of that sexual metamorphosis which repeatedly takes place. One could, as Georges Bataille did in his most profound works, attempt to equate the essence of sexuality with this metamorphosis, with this outer and inner exposure, this voluptuous nudity of the body and soul. The more shame a woman feels, the more she knows about this process. And the more she knows about this process, the more she craves it. The closer she comes to realizing her desire, the more intense her shame becomes. The vicious cycle is complete. Not until she has been given a green light, not until she is convinced that it is allowed and even desired, can she overcome her immense inhibitions. But then she goes all the way. Shame, which has many similarities with lust, transforms itself into the opposite when the occasion arises. An expression of shame in a woman's face is thus a charming and exhilarating advance notice of coming pleasures.

The shame wouldn't be so bad if it weren't implicitly linked to a fear of humiliation. On the one hand, humiliation is a consequence of the existing cultural conditions under which sexuality takes place, and on the other hand there is also the danger of humiliation in the sexual act itself. It begins physically as we change from an upright to a horizontal position. We instinctively respond to this motion with our most animalistic impulses, and this can result in the most beautiful ravaging of the scene of our lust. When such things occur in a society, which displays such repulsion and disgust for sexuality, then we are witness to a fatal collision of two very disparate elements – a collision that we'd rather avoid. Sexuality, which is open to a sensual, voluntary and controlled form of degradation, runs the risk of falling victim to a nasty form of degradation which no longer has anything to do with natural and erotic pleasure. It is the same thing that happens with violence. Sexual playfulness sometimes includes a small amount of violence and predatoriness, which is desired by both partners. It can be a great experience for the two of them, as long as it happens without any real violence, and those who have done it with one another enjoy being bound by a vow of trust. But they will be sorry if this playful form of inflicting pain gets out of hand and turns into real violence, which is an ever-present danger as long as we continue to inhibit and repress the free flow of feelings and communication. So where is the limit? When should we take risks and when should we restrain ourselves? Since we live together in such a stifling, moralizing, filthy and unaware atmosphere, where there is a real danger of degradation and violence, we are recommended to conceal our sexual desires. In order to bring about the affirmative transformation of shame, the basic idea of this book can be applied: We ourselves should create conditions and structures in accordance with what we want to live!

Shame is deeply anchored in both genders. Both would die of shame on the spot if their true thoughts and desires were to be revealed. This is an insight that we should always keep in mind: If everyone showed their true thoughts and desires, we would all shrink into the ground. The pious slogans and false pretenses would end. The tyranny of the cowardly "moral majority" over the "immoral minority" would be broken. The compulsion to distort and conceal would end since the admonishing stares of others would disappear. A whole world of hypocrisy and deceit would shrivel away! The world would be free to begin again. We human beings, children, adolescents and adults, women and men, could start over. But this time we won't blindly follow the traditions and roles that have been assigned to us, for they will have disappeared. Instead, we will live freely and intelligently according to our own knowledge and desires. This is the vision that I must keep in mind in order to write down the ideas of this book, since without a constructive purpose it would make no sense to say such things so clearly.

Women Over 40

Women who have reached the middle of life are at the peak of femininity. They are round, plump and desirable. A life of love is awaiting them, and it will continue until a very late age. They share their experiences about love with those who need to know, young women and young men, all those who are on the path of love.

That's how things could be if the world weren't so out of balance. No woman over 40 would even consider making herself look younger or getting a face-lift, since her attractiveness increases through natural aging. It would not occur to any woman to be ashamed of her sexual desires, for she loves and affirms sex. She would have no doubts about her societal role, for this would now be filled with a sense of love and responsibility. She is not afraid of getting older, because mature sexuality doesn't depend on an ideal body.

The reality, as we have created it, looks quite different. Women over 40 are either married or live alone. Nothing much happens in marriage; love has long since been swallowed up by daily routine. If they choose to live alone and could in fact start all over again, their way to happiness would be mostly blocked by social prejudices. In both cases they are forced to exist as asexual beings. Instead of living in the real sense, they are forced to play conventional roles. Instead of decorating themselves with the glitter of love, they decorate themselves with fashion. Instead of discussing real issues, they talk about the weather. Instead of making love, they find themselves baking cakes. The inner emaciation that they suffer from due to lack of love causes both their skin and mind to wilt. The flabs of today were once the curves promising an erotic love life. Even according to their own opinion they are no longer attractive enough for the dance of erotic love. They compare themselves with younger women and fail to notice that they have quite different qualities. When they get fed up with the consumer world and its various forms of satisfaction substitution, in their desperation they turn to religious or esoteric books. They occupy themselves with macrobiotics, natural healing, astrology and tarot (which isn't necessarily bad), with holistic forms of living and higher levels of consciousness. As part of a process of "sublimation," they divert energy away from their sexual impulses toward spiritual and aesthetic goals, and learn to view sacrifice as a virtue. There is no reason to object to any of these things; they simply don't reach the core of the matter, although they are the most intelligent form of survival given the circumstances. As Wilhelm Busch said, "Abstinence means taking delight in those things that we cannot attain." But these things would all be attainable, if we would begin – with all our powers of mind, love and truth – to break through the brutality of our sexual morals and create genuine alternatives for self-realization. We need a long time to understand sexuality – and life really only begins at 40.

Having reached life's fullest stage, a woman over 40 is, in the archetypal sense, a "mother figure" as well. This is the source of her profound spiritual energy and charisma. But unfortunately women at this age react in a strange way when this term is used. Instead of taking it as a compliment, they are dismayed. They don't realize what is really meant by this word. A woman's role as a mother figure does not contradict her role as a girlfriend or lover. A man who knows what love is does not react to this in such a way that he becomes infantile or impotent, but instead their love becomes more intense. The archetype of the mother figure is soft and yet very strong, natural, knowing, kind and comforting – something that one can rely on in life.

I would like to discuss these archetypal structures of our mind in more detail because there are truths about our cells and about creation to be found here which are much more profound than any societal nomenclature. Women over 40 make up the true spiritual center of any organic community. Their knowledge, truth and compassion determine how far the young adventurers can go without losing their way back to the nest. Their smile has more authority than the law. Through their consciously feminine role, they take care of the fundamental and organic aspects of life – the cellular processes of the community. The old images of the feminine role are not only false; they have been unjustly interpreted and exploited by men. This however does not warrant a return to the matriarchal system, since the historical development of the human species cannot be reversed; it can only go forward. But there are matriarchal structures and forces that go beyond all cultures and trends because they are linked to the universal polarity of creation.

The result of these links will be a transformation of the sexual and social function that a woman will face in future society. She will still have children, family and profession and will be aware of her own significance. But when she has gathered enough inner experience, she will continue to develop the ideas of love and communal living on a different scale – not just within her own private sphere, but on a public, political and wider human level. She will be admired and desired by young men because she has acquired so much knowledge and yet does not intimidate. She will not reject the archetypal desire of a young man for a mature woman; she will accept it with natural joy and responsibility. As all older women, she knows that the issue of so-called "incest" (as long as one does not fix this term narrowly to the biological family) is a basic question of human longing, and that young men seek her attention for this reason. She knows that her behavior can strongly influence the effects that this hidden desire has on a young man. She herself has had similar moving experiences with this issue and is aroused by the thought of sleeping with her "sons."

No direct sexuality between children and adults is meant. It is simply not appropriate for a child's development, nor would it appeal to adults with a fulfilled sex life. After childhood, everything is allowed which is desired by both partners, provided that it is communicated without false pretenses. All stages have a certain meaning and function in the development of mature sexuality. There are neither age restrictions (except those mentioned regarding children) nor any justifiable rules that can dictate which age groups are allowed to go to bed with one another and which are not. At the age of 76, Claire Goll made love to a 20-year-old and experienced sexual satisfaction for the first time. The film "Harold and Maude" shows a love life that breaks all age restrictions. Goethe, one of Germany's foremost intellectuals, married the 20-year-old Marianne Willemer at the age of 80. Wherever Eros finds its way, it always works wonders. Prefabricated moral regulations must give way. We should not pass judgment on those situations where Eros succeeds in breaking through the crusts of our life, we should try to learn and understand. Yet unexplored and unredeemed is the human being and the Earth, Nietzsche said. We are at a good place to begin this exploration and redemption – in the area of Eros, at the core of the matter.

Women over 40 have an important role to play in this process. They should know that there are enough men out there waiting for them. They should have the courage to prove that they are prepared. There must be a means of understanding, of getting the message across, and if there is not, then we must create it. Of course we can't all run around with a sign on our chest which reads, "I'm ready," but we can follow our intuition and search out those places where one is allowed to be "ready." There however may be, pleasing and meaningful signs of this willingness with which we could adorn ourselves.

The dreams and visions of a woman over 40 depend on how, consciously or unconsciously, she pictures getting older. These notions generally do not arise out of our authentic experience and intuition, but from the belief systems of our culture that are passed from generation to generation without question and are thus attained as an almost biological solidity and influence. These beliefs and tenets stem from an ancient Judeo-Christian culture and are stricken with an ingrained fear of carnal love. Today we are living in a period of historical change after which "there shall not be left one stone upon another." Hidden behind the apocalyptic events of our time, a human transformation is also in the offing which will bring with it new insights into the mental, spiritual and physical realities of our existence. They neither stem from a social era nor from a temporary fashion; they come from the ceaseless studio of creation. This is the source of laws that dictate freedom and not slavery, humanity and not morality, security and not desolation, healing and not sickness. Underlying these laws as well is another principle of growth and maturing. Getting older does not mean that energy is lost – it only becomes more complex. Getting older does not mean that the body dies; body cells are able to regenerate at every age, if the mind remains awake and alive. Not until the will to live begins to slack do the cells lose their energy. A 70-year-old who possesses an abundance of vital energy need not have the slightest fear of decline or deterioration. Life perpetually draws on its origins – life is perpetually renewable when they are maintained. If the first half of life comes to an end with toil and burden, the second can be started anew. We live in a boundless world, and it makes no sense to leave it until we have understood the world and ourselves.

Tenderness and the Intimacy Afterwards

Through a sexual encounter a feeling of pleasure arises that we prefer not to end immediately – we desire the "intimacy afterwards." Oh have we sinned in this respect, we men especially! A friend called me recently to talk about explosions and manslaughter and psychotherapy. Her boyfriend Mario had just left her hanging after a very nice time in bed – he simply got up and left. It was always like that, she said, and she couldn't stand it any more. Here I have no intention of condemning my fellow men; I would be much better off concentrating on my own shortcomings. But it's true that we have a way of passing from sex right back into our daily routine as if we had just brushed our teeth.

After a rapturous sexual encounter, a natural feeling of gratitude and tenderness generally follows. It gives us a lift which we would like to take with us into the world and into the day. A sexual encounter which ends at the moment of orgasm is like a spiritual coitus interruptus, since the process is broken off in the middle. The mental quality of sensual love, the joy that a man and a woman feel when they understand each other and make love to each other, is normally not fulfilled by merely performing the sexual act, it is only just awakened. It is often said that sexual union arises from tenderness. This is a limitation that does not necessarily correspond to the nature of Eros. Sexuality can arise from tender feelings, but it can just as well arise from the most bestial desires. Morally speaking, one is not better than the other. When it happens and it's good, a sort of natural tenderness develops. The lion licks its lioness.

There are circumstances under which sex becomes a routine, such as in marriage or in groups which have a conventional understanding of free love. There is nothing wrong with a quickie every now and then. Feel free to treat sex like brushing your teeth occasionally, as long as you don't have a bad taste in your mouth afterwards. But what goes on in that space of ten square feet between four bedposts mustn't be allowed to disappear from the rest of our daily life. Eros, even in its most carnal manifestation, has a fine and sensitive texture which longs for tenderness. It may however only be activated after we have reminisced over the experience with some distance. We certainly need a lot of conscious tolerance for one another in order to avoid being consumed by our anger over another's insensitivity. A man who leaves his wife like a stick-in-the-mud after the act would be shocked at his behavior if he could see what he was doing. If he weren't all caught up in his eternal film of performance and duty, if he weren't forced to compensate for his unfulfilled longing through work, if he hadn't got stuck in the initial stages of love, then he would immediately recognize the unconscious brutality of his actions. If he had room in his heart to develop sensual tenderness, then he would certainly do it, because tenderness is the continuation of sexuality by other means. To discover and welcome oneself as a sexual being and to keep love free of all outside pressures requires an open heart, which is not exactly at the top of the priority list of our male-dominated world.

For the woman, intimacy afterwards means being accepted. She experienced rejection from her father often enough as a child. She cannot and will no longer accept this kind of treatment. Bodily union is for the man often only a short excursion – for the woman it is home. As long as she doesn't get it, she will either rebel or despair. But when she gets it, she will understand and forgive everything. The intimacy afterwards determines how much "home" we can create between the genders and the extent to which we can release ourselves and be free for the next encounter. If sex has gone stale, it could be because it no longer changes anything. And sex won't change anything until we are able to open the sense organs of our soul, and not just our sex organs. Carnal love, a natural catalyst of warmth and security, sometimes becomes a catalyst of hardening. Once again we succeed in turning things around. At times we are simply left like children with tears in our eyes.

The Myth of Orgasm

There are a sizable number of men that have a special problem: they are unable to reach a climax during intercourse. They are so fixated on orgasm that it eludes them for this very reason. The woman senses this instinctively and is also unable to come. But it is the man's duty to satisfy the woman, right? And she is not satisfied until she has an orgasm, right? And so both of them get all bogged down and the whole thing ends in frustration.

I have nothing against orgasm. Wilhelm Reich's analysis of its importance for our health was certainly correct and was a strong blow at that time to our straightjacket attitudes toward behavior. But like all forms of inner release and fulfillment, orgasm is a phenomenon that occurs naturally without our conscious intervention, provided we don't hinder it through false fixation. Sexuality is about lust; it has nothing to do with competitive sport. This is quickly forgotten in a culture that places achievement and success above everything else in life. Even activities which are not competitive by nature, such as sexuality, yoga, tai chi, prayer and meditation, secretly become linked to performance. Can I or can I not? This question has unconsciously been pushed so strongly to the forefront that no room remains for actually experiencing the activity.

Zen monks used to give their disciples a "koan," an unsolvable mental problem, with which they were supposed to occupy themselves until they submitted to their fate – the insolvability of the problem. If they remained entangled in the problem too long, their master would sometimes throw them down the steps in order to enlighten them. It functions according to a very instructive principle, in which the pupils are distracted from their inner pressure to succeed by being surprised by an unforeseen event, causing an involuntary release which brings about enlightenment. Through a similar unforeseen event, it would be possible for our marathon couple to rid themselves of their stress and enhance their lust. We all know the feeling of release that results when we are freed from some entanglement by an intervening chance occurrence. Like all fulfilling things in life, fulfillment arises from its own sovereign casualness. Often enough, heaven itself has had to wait for us in front of our closed gates before it was casually allowed to enter.

Modern science has reduced sexuality to a physiological drive, a move which was certainly necessary in the intellectual confrontation with dusty morality and poetic euphemism. But once again it has thrown out the baby with the bathwater. Sexuality is by no means a mere gratification of a physiological urge; it is a voluptuous physical and spiritual contact between two human beings. Whether or not this contact leads to orgasm is beside the point. When I sit down to play the piano I think about more than just the powerful final chord of my recital. This will occur naturally when the time comes. It is exactly the same with free sexuality. By "free" I mean free of fear, free of the judging eye of our partner, free of the pressure to succeed and of the obligatory values of our upside-down conventions. The value and beauty of a sexual encounter does not depend on the quality of the orgasm; it depends on the quality of the contact. Sexuality is contact, or rather the continuation of contact by other means. Think of all the women who pretend to have an orgasm in order to please a man or to not appear frigid. Think of all the discussions and arguments that took place between men and women during the period of sexual liberation concerning the importance of whether or not they had an orgasm. I would give all men who have anything to do with this problem a simple piece of advice: go to bed with the woman, but don't ejaculate. What appears to be a loss is in fact none whatsoever. He is freed of stress and paves the way for a new experience. No woman will be angry about it; on the contrary, when the man stops toiling and sweating away, the woman will be able to comfortably and enjoyably find her own way.

Viktor Schauberger, the great natural philosopher, studied the forms of motion of water, fish and plants for years before pronouncing judgment on humans: "You move wrong." In nature and in all of its creations there is a form of motion which doesn't only expend energy, but which also generates energy. The energy drain that we suffer from performing our competitive sport of sex contrasts sharply with this natural principle of motion. Especially those who are already inhibited or over-stressed should try forgetting about performance for once and practice the laziest sex of which they are capable. Being lazy, doing nothing, relaxing and even going limp, drinking a glass of wine or reading a book together – these are all suitable and comfortable ways of avoiding the orgasm terror in bed.

The orgasm issue is made even more difficult by all the sentimental trash that is written about it in the name of poetry. Many people claim that orgasm is a nearly mythical union of two souls and two bodies which is heralded by an ecstasy which is so tremendous that "the limbs are dislocated and the head is twisted until tears of desire flow where the arse is split" (Dante). Such exaggeration is generally not a result of genuine experience; it is the product of a body which is sexually undernourished. Despite its blissful moments, sexuality is a very earthly and rational process. Its ecstasy may be heavenly, but it is still quite human. The myth of melting together, even until losing consciousness, mostly seems to stem from the fantasies of a blocked organism and not from reality. I do not want to deny that extraordinary, nearly transcendental moments of union can occur in sexuality, but these are extreme exceptions even in the love life of experienced lovers. Expecting an orgasm to have a transcendental nature or trying to turn it into "the measure of all things" is as extravagant and ridiculous as waiting for God to appear after your evening prayer. The myth of orgasm is thus connected to exaggerated fantasies of sexual union. These fantasies naturally lose their power as real love experiences occur in everyday life. Orgasm, which is a matter of only a few minutes or seconds, is not the central aspect of the issue of union between the genders. Much more important is the question of daily communication, understanding, cooperation and sensuality. Every now and then happiness does come in the form of a revelation in bed, but it still must be forged and molded in the workshop of life.

Just one more comment on the subject of orgasm: There are Taoist and Tantric masters who advise their male pupils to enjoy sexuality without orgasm. This allows Chi, the inner vigor which we require for physical and mental concentration, to remain alert for a longer period of time. I myself practice this before performing certain tasks and have never experienced any reduction in lust. The more the sexual contact itself becomes the source of pleasure, the less we are forced to rely on orgasm. Erotic art will enter a new stage when the artists of love stop allowing orgasm to occur as a biological reflex and begin to guide it and extend it in the spirit of Tantra. But that is a subject for the future temples of love, when the more urgent problems have been resolved.

Impotence – Energy with No Way Out

Impotence is a problem which goes deeper than it appears on the outside. All of us have experienced it at one point or another, and many of us still do. Both men and women are affected, although it is more readily apparent among men. Impotence is an ugly word, even worse than frigidity when applied to a woman. It makes one feel labeled and branded. Impotence is a phenomenon which occurs when the organism reacts with fear toward sexuality and/ or when the mind places the sexual process in false relation to thoughts about performance and "ability." Concerning this issue of ability and obligation regarding sexuality, I would like to quote a humorous passage from the book Rettet den Sex [Save Sexuality]:

> "When someone is impotent, it is because he believes he must be able to do something which in reality he is not required to be able to do – and which he could do if he stopped thinking about it in terms of ability and obligation, can and must.
>
> The assumption of having to be able to do something which in reality one does not have to be able to do, because one is naturally able to do it when one doesn't think about it, leads in most cases to disruptions of natural abilities. Those who are truly unable are subsequently reinforced even more in their false assumption concerning ability and obligation. In this way sex is turned into a competitive sport which can have no winner. If someone is unable to do it and sees no light at the end of the tunnel, he still should not take it too seriously. Above all, he should not pretend that he can when he cannot. Those who can and who we love are occasionally those who cannot, but who accept their inability in a charming way without sweating over it."

Occasional impotence is a normal reaction to the stressful conditions of our time. The real form of suffering is the case of impotence occurring as a long-term or structural ailment. It occurs even when both partners have a very strong desire. Structural impotence is often a symptom of sexual blockage, for example when the man comes before it has really started, or when he can't get it up because all the congested currents of energy obstruct each other and can't reach the necessary organs. The worst thing about impotence is the way it affects inner processes that are connected to it. The man senses the coming disaster and tries to escape it. While considering the appropriate moves, he keeps one eye on the thoughts of his partner and the other on the state of his penis. Secretly he checks and discovers to his dismay that it is still too limp for penetration. He may try to get it up by thinking of erotic fantasies, but then he has doubts because they have nothing to do with his partner. He is entangled in a tricky game and would be very happy if the telephone were to ring – saved by the bell. He could invent some pretext in order to answer the phone and then escape from the difficult situation for a while. There are occasional erotic moments which raise his hopes again, but they are only fleeting sensations. The woman, usually a source of lust, slowly becomes the source of a serious threat (of which she knows nothing). Despite all of this, appearances must of course be kept up. She is lying there, still quite desirable, but I desire nothing more; I'm only looking for a way out. I know that she is unsatisfied and that she had expected more. Should we talk to one another? About what? That would only make things worse. So I just pretend that everything is ok. I kiss her; we continue to hold each other until she asks me if we want to smoke a cigarette. I gladly accept.

That's more or less what the experience called "impotence" feels like on the inside. A man can deal with it a few times, and a woman as well, but fear gradually builds up that the next encounter will end in a similar way. And it is always this anxiety that causes it to happen in the first place. A self-fulfilling prophecy of sorts, it becomes a vicious cycle that is impossible to escape. He might have truly loved this woman; a genuine, sensual, maybe even long-lasting friendship could have arisen. But the way things went, they could only part without having achieved anything. How many farewells have been said in this way! How many opportunities have been lost! How many dreams have dissolved under the pressure of those forces that stand in the way of sensuality? Sexual need is equally divided between both genders. A woman who is afraid of being frigid must run the gauntlet each time in the same way as an impotent man. The only difference is that she has more possibilities to conceal her feelings because she does not need to take an active role. And there is a lot that must be concealed here, since words are so painful. The woman as well usually lacks the experience and the courage to help out in such a situation, and in addition she generally expects the man to take the initiative in sexual matters, which is not entirely without good reason. The sexual landscape of today has contours which practically no human being can come to terms with. Behind it is an obscure world of concealment and silence. If there is a password for the liberation of sensual love, then perhaps it is this: Get your bodies to speak and start right where you are.

The issue of impotence begins long before we land in bed. It doesn't actually have anything to do with sex – it's merely the area in which it most strongly manifests itself. We are all impotent at that moment when we become internally blocked through the presence and gaze of others. Who isn't familiar with the precarious situation of standing at a urinal and not being able to piss because someone else is standing next to you? Isn't it interesting that I can't piss when someone else is there who might be watching me? This example can easily be extrapolated. I can't eat, sing, dance, etc. because other people are watching! There has been one great expert in this field of impotence: the French philosopher Jean Paul Sartre. In his book Being and Nothingness he writes, "The gaze of others is the hidden death of my freedom of action." Corresponding to the general principle of performance there is a general principle of judgment. In this way, life always goes on in front of the critical and judging eyes of others – especially in bed. Nobody can avoid this fate, not even the most dignified statesmen of our time. Even the best and most handsome of us can be flops in bed. The superstar Sylvester Stallone for instance had to put up with women saying he was a wimp and that he couldn't get it up.

When the penis remains small and limp when it should be big and hard, one of the most embarrassing thoughts for a man arises: you're a wimp. When a woman comes along and confirms this label, then a catastrophe is already preprogrammed. The pain which results from such humiliation and shame goes so deep that it often cannot be overcome without alcohol, the consequences of which are the everyday atrocities of our time that we read about in the newspapers. There is nothing else with which a man is so strongly identified as with his penis and its performance. He must use it to prove himself; it can be his pride or his downfall. It makes or breaks his bonds of friendship with men; it is his link to the world of women; it is his measuring stick, his divining rod, his magic wand and his ID card. It is what determines whether we feel happy or unhappy, even if we have coated it with a soothing layer of humor and mild philosophy.

Impotence is a kind of brainteaser which reveals a certain mode of existence. You miss the goal because you are too obsessed with its realization. It's like driving a car. If you sit tensely behind the wheel and concentrate too much on the traffic, you may lack the necessary lightness at the moment where you most need it in order to react correctly. The decisive moments in life come when you least expect them, when you don't try to force them.

Hermann Hesse said, "As long as you try to stalk happiness, you are not mature enough to be happy, when all things could be yours." There is an unusual book that deals with the subject of potency and impotence in the field of archery in which the correlations between a too narrow goal fixation and the corresponding failure to reach the goal are thoroughly expounded. The book is by Eugen Herrigel and is called Zen and the Art of Archery. In it he describes the strange method of learning that he had to undergo with a Zen monk before he was able to hit his target. At the beginning he was so fixated on drawing the bow, positioning the arrow correctly and releasing it at the right moment, that he inevitably missed the target. Not until he "forgot" his intentions was he able to hit the bull's eye.

Success often depends less on the amount of effort we exert and more on the extent to which we "forget" our exertion. The joy that we experience during a sexual encounter comes from the situation itself, not through carrying out a planned and deliberate action.

A man may be impotent because he gets stuck in a phase where he concentrates too much on the individual techniques and thus loses touch with the act as a whole. He does his best and is still unable. The harder he tries, the worse he does. Then he may go to a doctor or to a drugstore to get something which enhances his sexual potency. And if he believes in it strongly enough, it may even work. But it's like the faith healing of the holy water at Lourdes: It's not the medicine that cures you; it's your own belief in its power that allows you to influence unconscious patterns of behavior.

Impotence usually does not arise from any sexual weakness; it arises from bottled up sexual energy, which finds no release because it is guided by false thoughts. It gets stuck somewhere along the way before it even reaches the genitals. It often causes the mind to get mixed up, and it is then unable to send sensible and coherent impulses to the body. When the command center is confused, the body is also confused. When the mind sends contradictory information, then the dick as well has a hard time deciding what to do. This in turn profoundly upsets the mind, and generally leads to a vicious cycle, resulting in the dick going on strike. The problem of impotence is usually solved by itself when some occurrence or discovery within the conscious mind brings about a shift or turn which itself enables a solution to be found.

I love the story of the bound elephant. A young Indian elephant is tied to a tree so that he cannot get away. He is stuck to this tree every day, and all his efforts to escape are futile. He convinces himself of the hopelessness of his situation, and in the end he even accepts his fate. One day the guard comes and cuts the rope without the elephant noticing. The elephant however knows nothing of his good fortune and continues to remain next to the tree in the assumption that he is still tied up. Occasionally he thinks about his situation and considers ways of freeing himself, but the more he concentrates on this problem, the stronger he feels that even more chains are being put on him. Thus he listens to reason; he becomes sensible and gives up. He convinces himself that there is nothing wrong with being tied up to a tree. Life goes on normally in this way and he forgets the whole thing, until one day he suddenly sees a strong and beautiful elephant standing in front of him which appears to be enjoying its freedom and vitality to the utmost. In this instant an image shoots across his mind and he sees a picture of himself enjoying the same freedom and vitality. Without any hesitation or deliberation, he surges forward to greet his companion. The old spell was simply gone. The spontaneous self-identification with the new image was stronger than the bond that linked him to the film from the past. Without this experience he would have kept torturing himself needlessly for years to come. But life, especially human life, is full of such eventualities. Whenever our turbulent feelings come into contact with the higher forces of life, it is always possible to change direction. As we are not elephants, we can use our minds to prepare ourselves for this change.

Sexual Hopelessness of the Organism

Sexual energy is an integral part of the universal energy of creation. Its influence is not limited to the sexual glands and organs; it affects all the cells and physiological processes of the whole organism. The entire organism, not just part of it, is a sexual being equipped with basic sexual functions which operate independently of the urge to reproduce and propagate the species. But in a way reproduction is biological evidence that sexuality is at the origin and beginning of all things, since it is necessary for the preservation of the species.

Every sexual disruption causes a disturbance in the functioning of the organism as a whole, including our intellectual and ethical faculties. Almost every psychosomatic illness is to some extent a result of blocked or disrupted sexual energies. Wilhelm Reich established the validity of the connection on a theoretical basis and proved it clinically. When people feel weak, tired, afraid, unhappy or depressed, it is almost always because they are in conflict with their sexual nature. No diet can restore the inner balance, unless it is in harmony with the sexual circulation; and no form of natural healing can repair the damage caused by the continual sexual blockage of the organism, unless it also does something to remove this blockage.

The spiritual source of almost all illnesses is found in the false application of our powers of recognition to the meaning and function of sexual energies in human life. The difference between human and animal sexuality is that in humans it is not only a matter of reproduction, but also a process of transformation. Sexual energies help to heal the mind by tearing down the borders of the body. **Due to our mental and spiritual nature, any human being has a thousand times more sexual appetite than any other animal.**

Sexual energies in the form of pure, liberated lust are the best kind of biological and psychological powers of healing that exist. Illness is a result of a blockage and disruption in the circulation of sexual energies. The most important task of a new form of medicine, if it is to overcome the old way of thinking in the epoch of unredeemed

Eros and teach us to make use of our natural "resources" and healing powers, will be found in the unblocking and freeing of sexual energies. All therapy centers and health resorts could greatly increase their healing success rate if they gave their patients a real opportunity to release their sexual energies.

I have had many patients in my therapeutic practice who were plagued with everything under the sun, including chronic obesity, underweight, goiters, eye problems, migraine headaches, abdominal abscesses, defective lymph glands and kidneys, psychosomatic illnesses of all kinds and cancer. After initial attempts with various methods such as psychotherapy, group therapy and postural integration, I was forced to change the fundamental direction of my work. The subject of sex had come up so often while working with my patients that any therapy which did not consciously deal with sexual energies seemed meaningless to me. Sexual energy itself is a healing energy par excellence. It belongs to the self-healing powers of the human organism and can be used for the healing process to the same extent that it is released from its blockages. Healing is understood here as the sexual unblocking of the organs.

Infections, whether temporary or chronic, are almost always an expression of congested energy. This built-up energy arises when sexual stimulations cannot be relieved in a natural way because they conflict with morality, with fear and shame, with the structures of marital and family life. Due to the consequent attempts of avoidance and repression on the part of the patient, this dammed-up sexual energy then gives rise to secondary symptoms, so that congestions and infections appear in places on the body which have no clear connection with sexuality. They can lead to a goiter on the throat, inexplicable pressure behind the eyes, chronic bladder infections, asthma, and much more. The energy congestion often latches on to that place on the body which at that moment is playing a central role in a sexual conflict, and it is often a symbolic role – one says, "I don't want to hear anything more about that," so one suffers from hearing problems. "I don't want to think about that anymore," so one gets a headache when the subject comes up again, consciously or unconsciously.

I have observed a phenomenon in chronically obese women that I was spontaneously able to understand. They had a continual sexual appetite which they could not satisfy, and as an alternative to this they began to eat. Orality and sexuality are very close to each other. It is because of their gluttony that they got fat, and they knew it. But instead of controlling their appetite, they intentionally continued to eat. This reaction is easily comprehensible. If this world and these men are so shitty, then 'I'll just stuff myself with food!' Often it is a simple, understandable and friendly anger, which causes the body to swell up. But much more often it is a latent variety of perpetual anger that is responsible. In both cases, the anger and the accompanying bodily symptoms are a result of chronic sexual hopelessness of the organism.

Rudolf Steiner, whose mental activity reached a rather high level of intellectual perception despite his ignorance of the workings of sexuality, once said that illness arises where there is too much soul in the body. This statement gets to the core of the matter. Through the hopelessness of sexual and psychosexual energies, the organism is pumped up with all sorts of internal conflicts. Collisions resulting from energy transformation are always linked to corresponding thoughts and emotions. The organic, hormonal and vegetative processes of the body are to a certain extent connected to the corresponding mental processes, and vice versa. This results in a big psychophysiological mess from which neither the body nor the mind can free itself. Wherever mental and spiritual energies are so completely absorbed by the body, they are no longer available for an unbiased gaze into the world and a free manner of participation in its events, for perception, discovery and appreciation.

Body and soul belong together; but it is still important for some forms of therapy to temporarily free the body from too much influence of the mind and cleanse it. This release can be brought about by all great ideas, if they are genuine, by all new and great experiences and above all by sensual love. It is, like any true religious experience, the superior force that throws out the goblins and brings the organism into balance. It possesses an enormous healing potential granted to us by nature at birth.

The human organism of our day is in a state of sexual despair almost everywhere. We can only cope with it by diverting our energies to other activities, such as sport, career, culture and war. This is however not a form of healing. True healing consists in finding a positive outlet for this estranged and congested sexual energy. This is not a mechanical act; it requires a change in both the inner and outer life situations. Even when his sexual therapy was nearing success, Wilhelm Reich's cancer patients would usually relapse if they were unable to find sexual fulfillment in their outer life. Healing through sexual therapy is, in the long term, hardly possible under the existing societal conditions. Despite the best therapeutic efforts, new symptoms will appear again after a while, perhaps in completely different organs. Sexual decongestion and permanent healing of the organism can only succeed if the patient has the opportunity after the therapy to build up a new sexual life without repression or the compulsion to lie. This task goes beyond the conventional medical sphere, yet it is still the most important medical task of our time. The subject of healing can no longer be limited to the traditional medical area; it must be extended to include our entire sexual existence and must create new possibilities of experience for this existence. We need very concrete institutions where patients and others who want to regenerate themselves have the opportunity to find sexual fulfillment which life generally does not offer. Such a sanctuary for sexual lust and healing could replace ten modern clinics.

Am I Attractive Enough?
Reflections on Sexual Attraction

Sexual attraction is simply there; it doesn't need to be fabricated. In principle, every woman is sexually attractive to men, simply because she is a woman. And the same applies the other way around. One should instead ask how it is even possible to lose attractiveness. But we no longer need to pose this question, since it was sufficiently discussed in the preceding chapters.

When women ask about their sexual attractiveness, they usually mean their outward appearance, figure, hairstyle, make-up, etc. Let's talk about appearances for a moment. The female figure is always attractive, when it is recognizable as such. What is less attractive is what women do to their figure under the pressure of fashion and modern styles. With their shoulder pads, unsexy pants and cool look, they are love-killers incarnate. Their drawn-in waists, which are supposed to be a sign of beauty, reveal to us that no more vital sexual currents are flowing, not from bottom to top or from top to bottom. The "bellylessness" of the feminine ideal of beauty goes hand-in-hand with the chic looking emptiness of the faces. I don't know why so many women take part in this fashion fair; it's not even a vanity fair any more, because if you were vain, you would at least want to be pretty as well. I don't understand why women who weigh over 135 pounds despise their bodies. They don't realize how beautiful they are and often invest the most absurd amount of will power to lose just one pound. With all of their might they try to remove the most beautiful spots, which are like love cushions on their hips, bottoms and legs. What should a man take hold of, if there's nothing left of her? When a man gazes at a woman, his eyes always function a little bit like an extended sense of touch, like tentacles. A woman is in any case attractive at that moment when a man feels desire to touch her.

I thus request of all women that you keep your soft spots and plump curves, even if they are a bit lavish. You should know that there are many men who delight in and crave such a figure.

A full feminine body of 165 pounds together with a personable face is in any event more sexually attractive than the lifeless and factory-made figures of the fashion world. Perhaps you do not have the qualifications for such deep professions such as a model or a mannequin, but in bed you will discover other joys, as long as you are not too ashamed of your splendor. After having made this personal declaration of taste, which I share with many experienced men, I would like to go into the question of attractiveness in more depth.

"What is beauty?" When asked this question in a TV interview, Josef Beuys laughed and answered, "Beauty is the glitter of truth." This answer provides us with food for thought which can be applied to sexual beauty as well. What is most important about beauty is not its embodiment of outward aesthetic characteristics, but that it is the reflection of an inner disposition. We often meet people who are by no means beautiful in the external sense of the word, and yet we are spellbound by their irresistible sexual aura. They just have that certain something.

A woman stands in front of the mirror in the morning and makes herself pretty. She compares her external appearance with the desired, idealized picture she has of herself. There are a few too many wrinkles, there is a little bit too much fat, but with a few cosmetic adjustments the flaws can be corrected. She is pretty. She will go into the city and feel the men look at her. And they really do think she's pretty and attractive, at least at first sight. But is that enough for the second encounter, and is that enough if they get to know each other better? Isn't her bottom too large, aren't her breasts too small, isn't her gait a little bit too clumsy? She constantly worries about her outward appearance. She may have a relatively big nose; perhaps her malicious girl friends call it a "ski jump." She has therefore gotten used to lying in bed with a man in such a way that he is unable to see her profile. The worries she has about her looks absorb a large part of her attention, and part of her charisma is swallowed up by her habit of viewing herself through the eyes of others. The more she gets caught up in this narcissistic exhibitionism, the more she loses sexual attractiveness. On the contrary, if she stops worrying, she will begin to get a feeling for her sexual radiance and attractiveness, which has a lot to do with being "free from oneself." These characteristics of "naturalness" and "openness" belong to those basic qualities which we appreciate in any person. But they aren't enough for the phenomenon we call "sex appeal" – sexual resonance must have a different source.

Beauty is not only the glitter of truth; it is the glitter of love as well. All those who possess the energy of love are beautiful. This basic quality is visible even if wrinkles of worry and self-doubt mar their faces. We love them because they radiate love, and we can warm ourselves in their presence. This is an element of erotic attraction as well, but there is more.

Another source of sexual attraction is a person's "authentic" character. To what extent are we true to ourselves? To what extent do we think our own thoughts and reveal our own true feelings? This is where it gets hot. We always notice people who have an independent, self-determined character. They possess a sovereign force of attraction in both the mental and sexual arenas. Authenticity is sexy. The saying "she loves him because he uses his head" is an opinion I share. When the true essence of one person comes into resonance with that of another, a strong attraction necessarily arises. Jean Paul Sartre and Simone de Beauvoir are an example of two people who were joined in such a way.

But true sex appeal involves more. It is something that I like to call "sensual knowledge." It consists of a face, a gesture and an exchange of words; and even if it is only implied, it invokes a peculiar and erotic fascination. It is already present to some degree in children, though still in a rudimentary and unconscious form. "She'll really be something," we think to ourselves, referring to a certain very discreet and intimate quality, which is the pronouncement of an erotic being. Men and women are sexually attractive because they possess an erotic self-awareness. If that is not the case, then they have yet to discover it. But once they begin to sense this self-awareness, it no longer requires any additional discovery. A person who is capable of living without vanity but with erotic self-awareness radiates a sensual refinement which we always react to erotically. Sexuality is a question of resonance. According to the laws of physics, one body can transfer vibrations to another if the second body has the same resonating frequency as the first, with the result that both bodies vibrate together on a similar wavelength. Sexuality functions likewise, and has much more freedom when not just physical resonance is present, but also mental resonance. Sexuality is sparked by physical stimuli, but the only true basis for sexual attraction is formed in the mind. We possess very erotic mental structures, and very un-erotic ones as well. The most beautiful physique turns pale when you place a wooden head on top of it. But far less beautiful bodies begin to blossom when they are guided by an erotic mind. You can recognize the "initiates" by their physiognomy and the way they carry their body.

What is it that men love about young girls who they ignorantly call "Lolita"? They crave that certain combination of sensuality, innocence and emerging awareness. So what is it that they like about mature women? They like the combination of sensuality, naturalness and knowledge. What is it that women especially like about men? They like the combination of genuine thinking, energy and sensual knowledge. In the end it is always quite astonishing to what extent the body can free itself from the contemporary standards of beauty once it is filled with mental and physical vitality.

An Appeal to Women

There are many women who have the fortune, or perhaps the misfortune, of possessing the aura of the "beautiful woman." They know that they are considered beautiful, they are aware of the acceptance they receive from men and they take advantage of this by presenting themselves seductively, but they have already had bad experiences with it. They entice, but when someone takes the bait they say "no," which only enhances their power. When a woman looks especially attractive, I can usually see the "no" already written on her lips. Here we are obviously dealing with a women's parlor game which is very effective in the zoological garden of our society. The more a woman says "no," the more she is desired. The will to Eros has been transformed into the will to power. Women like this who are desired by everyone do not derive their vital energy from love, but instead they live from the projections of others. The cool domination that they are thus able to exercise can generally be maintained only as long as their beauty holds. Beauty, if it is to be permanent, must be based on love, not power. The results can be seen 20 years later, when the signs of loneliness and disappointment begin to appear in their faces. The game wasn't worthwhile after all. And yet very young women are imitating it. The rules are: Don't reveal your feelings. Let the men sweat a little bit; keep them in suspense. Show them that you're not easy to get! Behind this proud sort of self-rape is of course a falsely oriented man's world, which really does believe that a woman has no worth if she is easy to get. Women emancipate themselves simply by molding this nonsense to suit their own needs. The emancipation of women thus degenerates into a mere counterpart of the existing male structures. Women do not attempt to free themselves from this situation; instead they conform to these structures by simply complementing them. True emancipation of women would involve the opposite – not complying with these sexually hostile structures, but breaking through them. In this way we see how such structures develop in the sexual network of our society, where Eros is forcibly distanced from love. Sex and love thus take different paths – a circumstance that has led to the present schizophrenia in the relationship between the genders. One is continually confronted with two opposing signals: "come," and "go away." Modern schizophrenia researchers have even cited this irreconcilable "double bind" situation as a cause of mental illness, which already begins in childhood. As long as this structure dominates the forms of erotic life that are publically displayed, there can be no peace among the genders. This type of psychological warfare leaves no room for winners; everyone is a victim.

Obstacles to love have been created by men, but it will require an initiative by women to overcome them. Women should not react to male narrow-mindedness with militant feminism, for this would only be a blind echo of men; they should instead find their own, new way.

I have a request to all women who are interested in saving love: when you meet a man you like, forget the stereotypic "no." Don't turn to ice behind your prudish beauty – get involved and help to improve the situation. There are certainly old school men with whom it's not worthwhile trying, since they immediately misunderstand even the slightest "yes." But when you meet someone you like, make contact; be a little bit more insistent. If you're interested in someone, let him know by sending out clear signals. If a man already has a woman at his side, don't let that stop you. None of us are "taken" to such an extent that we are unable to look at anyone else. The woman on his side is the same as you. If she loves and desires him, then she will understand why you have the same wish. That can be no reason to drive each other away. We love each other, but we don't possess each other, since we are not masters and slaves. When I say "we" I mean all of us who think the same way and want to work in this direction.

There is no reason for going to bed with a man if you don't feel like it, but there is also no reason for not doing it when you do feel like it. No woman has any sexual obligation to any man. That must stop as well. There are no obligations at all in this domain. But neither is there any obligation to behave in a decent and proper way. It would be quite refreshing to see a little bit more "sin," although I know that is sometimes difficult because it requires the right men. When I observe men whistling at you on the street corners I can certainly understand that it is not easy for a woman to keep cool in such situations. You need a lot of artistic talent to say "no" ten times and yet remain open. I am familiar with this sort of permanent harassment through stories told to me by my closest female friends. What I liked most about their stories was that they were able to maintain a certain attitude in which their "no" was not a result of arrogance or struggle, but rather a result of the unfortunate fact that the solidarity you offered was either misused or misunderstood by the man. And yet that was no reason for them to hate men or to make the derogatory remark that "men only want one thing," which is true anyway.

Unfortunately, the men you would like to have are usually not as pushy as the others. When one of your chosen is too shy and reserved, help him with a little gentle persistence in order to overcome his barriers. Use your seductive powers; small signs usually suffice. Don't let passive waiting mess things up. We have admired your beautiful shapes long enough from a distance. You have felt the covetous gaze of a thousand men's eyes directed at you. Take it seriously, don't complain, abandon your innocence. If you only knew how much unredeemed desire you evoke in the hearts of men! If you only knew that these crude advances are usually just a result of helplessness! It isn't always a sign of humiliation or hidden contempt for women if a man is too pushy or uses the wrong words. It isn't always easy to remain charming and relaxed when you've had to deal with years of frustrated desire. It's the same for you women. Help to bring about a positive solution to this problem. Let us transform the pain of unredeemed desire into a real possibility for mutual joy. The flash that hits us when we occasionally catch sight of each other cannot simply be allowed to fade away. We have made love to you long enough in our thoughts. Now it's time to work together so that your dream and our dream can meet and come to life. Life is too beautiful to be wasted on anxieties and secrecies. We love your splendor and your souls; we love your shame and your shamelessness. Like you, we want love, and we want to complement each other to get the best out of it. I can see that our desire for each other is evolving into new feelings of gratitude and solidarity. Stop the war and we shall do the same. Forever. Amen.

It has Nothing to do with Sex?

It's one o'clock in the morning. I'm sitting at my desk, I feel good, and I can see the blinking of the digital clock on the TV set. At the moment I don't need sex; I need a cigarette (I only smoke at night). I enjoy the hours during which I am free from this sexual phantom. I have the same thoughts as anyone else. What in the world will others think about us when we are at the end of our lives? That we didn't have enough sex? Out there the moon is orbiting the Earth and a whole universe is glowing beyond it. I know neither where it came from nor where it's going, but isn't that a more sublime reality than ours? Why must we human beings always clutch to the same things that enchain us and torment us in such suffocating conditions? Have art and philosophy only arisen as a result of the repression of our other drives? I don't think I'm repressing anything at the moment, but right now I feel closer to Vincent van Gogh than to Bukowski. I must cast my spiritual anchor in these other areas. Please don't touch me now; I need fresh air. There are times when I can't bear to hear the word sexuality, although much of what you say is true. But the same god who created your heaven also created iron with which to destroy it. I know of no paradise that was not destroyed before being completed. This goes to show that our dialectical world is so full of contradictions that it is impossible to place all your bets in one basket. Don't touch me; I haven't finished yet! I myself love a woman, and I still love her today, because we have agreed on other things besides the priority of sexuality. Our marriage is not a ghetto, and neither is it a renunciation of the many other forbidden fruits. Or do you think it's a lie and nothing but a lie when I say that we still love each other? Your wisdom is too clever, too refined, too young, too all embracing and too fast for such a lofty goal. Every runner must stop and take a rest once in a while in order to see what else is going on in the world. Incredible things are really happening. The universe consists of more than just lovesickness.

The argument seen from the other side: But let's not change the subject. Why do you only refer to the genital act when you talk about sexuality? There is so much more to it which can be just as beautiful and just as important. All of us are at a certain level, and when we have passed through all of them, we often start over again. When Henry Miller was so old that he could no longer do it, he discovered a new love for Brenda. He wrote her daily love letters like a schoolboy. His soul was filled with something different than in his genital "Opus Pistorum." But was it less meaningful because of that? Many of us have not attained the inner constitution that we desire. So we should not rush into sex. Before the stimulation reaches the penis, it should pass through the eyes, the mouth, the heart and the stomach. All of them have their own spiritual qualities, their own theme, their own needs. They are all in resonance with the world and would like to remain so. Your kind of sex is like a one-way street downhill, but another direction is also possible. Goethe said "O, in my bosom live two souls. But I am only aware of one of them." So what makes you think you can decide on something that concerns all of us? I consider the traditional mythology of our culture as a mature thesis, and your theory as an intelligent antithesis. But I can't believe in either one of them.

Then the other voice spoke again, in a way that could have been me, about many other things – about the facets of voluptuous desire, about the emanations of the soul. He spoke about the troubadours and the minnesingers, about homosexual love, about the diversity of being, about Siddhartha and Hermann Hesse. He was obviously moved by the spirit of those thoughts which oppose every definitive judgment, since our knowledge of the world doesn't allow it. His thoughts seem so similar to mine that I would prefer to save myself the trouble of a controversy. And yet my mind is somewhere else. My imaginary conversation partner would have spoken differently if he had realized what sort of spiritual background these new thoughts came from. They are new, but he thinks that he already knows them. He has chosen a very clever and very refined way of immunizing himself from life.

That as well might be wisdom. It is wisdom for stoics and philosophers, but not for human beings subject to the storms of Eros. Whoever considers the ideas of this book carefully will notice that the arguments of our stoicism have certainly been taken into account.

Sometimes it really doesn't have anything to do with sex, nor with love. We may encounter decisive situations of such fundamental nature that our inner instinct regards the whole sexual issue as an obstacle, and justifiably so. At that moment one simply has something else to do. It's not a matter of repression or inner deception; it's a friendly request of an inner voice which is pointing in a very different direction. We should not allow ourselves to fall victim to all this turmoil concerning issue number one. Above all we should not think that something is wrong just because we happen to be preoccupied with completely different things. The world is much too complex for us to restrict ourselves just to this one subject, and the solutions generally arise by chance, not as a result of any fixed concentration.

The message is about liberation, not about any new fixation, and the shortest way of solving a problem is often to take a detour. The readers who feel themselves put under pressure by so much sexuality should consider that I am forced to place the issue of sexuality in the forefront, due to the entirety of my experience. I know that many people are less affected by the issue than others are at the moment. We should not make comparisons, nor should we gauge ourselves by the values of a new theory of sexuality.

I don't want to establish any new authorized values; I want to promote understanding. As regards the current living situation of many people, the question of love may be more important than the question of sex. They should simply pick out of this book those thoughts that they can productively use. It is an unnecessary habit of the human mind to consider all things controversial which do not immediately correspond to our mode of thinking. The content of any train of thought leading to sexual humanism will thus not be viewed as a means of enriching one's own potential, but as a danger which must be thwarted. Like robots with an ingrained consciousness of duty and obligation, we can only liberate ourselves by force.

People who feel they are making no progress in love should not worry too much about it. If we were to wait for our desires to be fulfilled before we began living, we would probably never begin living. Security in matters of love often arises when we recognize and accept the task that is offered to us within a certain human network. By way of some sort of life occupation or profession, everyone generates an organization of inter-human relationships which, if we act sensibly, arouses our mental and sexual powers of love. When we find our issue in life, we also find love. At times, sexual attraction develops on its own, when we pay the least attention to it.

PART III:
PRIMAL PAIN AND JEALOUSY

Primal Pain

What happens in the soul of a one-year-old child when it is given away to foster parents? What does it mean for a child to be abandoned? I'll make it short since the subject of primal pain is too cruel to dwell on for too long. At some time or another, usually as a child, we have all experienced such monstrous pains of separation, which have molded us right down to the core. If this were not the case, there would be no such thing as jealousy. The rage that we feel as adults is a reminiscence of past trauma. The first experience of primal pain we have is certainly that of being left alone. Primal pain has other sources as well, such as meaningless punishment for wrongdoings that were innocently committed. In their fight against love, sex and truth, individuals who are bound by tradition have developed such an inner vulnerability that they are unable to prevent themselves from passing on their wounds to others. A chain reaction of pain, injury and suffering is set in motion, which is unconsciously passed on from parents to children, from generation to generation. Are parents even aware of what they do to their children when they ignore or punish their attempts at affection? Does a mother know how much she is adored and desired by her three-year-old son? Does a father know the extent to which he is a model and demigod for his child, and how deeply his/her life can be affected by his actions? In most cases they have no idea at all, since they themselves were brought up in a similarly harsh manner, or they are so embroiled in their own unsolved problems that they are unaware of what is happening around them. No special theory is needed to explain the origin of primal pain. It is sufficient to look at what has happened to so many children in so many families up to now. The shocking number of cases of child abuse, as atrocious as it may be, is only the tip of the iceberg – and all this in the midst of "civilized," democratic and prosperous nations. Child abuse is a visible and concrete form of injury to the child. The traumatic experience that is more often connected to primal pain, however, is the result of continual and latent disregard of the child through indifference and apathy, through obsessive consumption of junk food, mass media, etc. Our Brave New World has developed its own methods of permanently stigmatizing children in a subtle way.

All of us who have experienced primal pain, either during childhood or later, use any means to try to escape from it and never again encounter it. We instinctively attempt to avoid all situations, people and events that could remind us of our dreadful trauma. We build a protective wall around the wound, in the same way an area infected by tuberculosis does, so that no one can get to it and stir it up. Since these wounds are almost always inflicted in the realm of love and sexuality, protective walls and avoidance mechanisms are very common here. We loved someone once, but we were so horribly deceived, disappointed or punished that we can never love again. In fact, this renunciation of love often occurs in early childhood. Everyone has seen the faces of two-year-olds who feel that they have been treated unjustly or who cannot understand the adult world. We witness an immense power of despair, but also an immense power of will. The child is already forging plans for revenge at an age when adults only think of it as being cute. Since we all originate from such structures, we are branded children as well, and we are especially branded in the domain of love. Whenever a child's trust is met with an adult's indifference, fractures occur in the development of love which cannot be easily healed. So-called traumatic patterns are instilled in us. They usually remain with us for the rest of our lives, and read like this: Be careful when you're in love. Don't get mixed up in it; you'll probably just be deceived or abandoned again. A fateful film, made up of love, revenge and the fear of loss, emerges in our subconscious. Love as it exists today in our society is to a large extent dictated by the content of this horror film.

It is more than understandable why many people want nothing to do with adventures in love and Eros under these circumstances. Instead they use avoidance strategies to maneuver their love ships carefully around the cliffs of love. They may choose a partner for life whom they don't really love or even desire, but who offers enough flexibility so that they don't become completely stultified. Or they may develop an altruistic ethic of giving and caring, since their most burning wish, that of receiving love, was never fulfilled. Or they simply condemn everything they love, which is one of the most popular methods today. I myself have experienced it, and I see it in others as well: The more you love and admire someone, the more you feel it necessary to humiliate him. Making contact by way of rejection is the motif of this mysterious ritual. I could go on and make a very long list of these strange customs. While working and thinking in Marxist circles for seven years, I could never shake off the suspicion that for many of my comrades this work was a means of distraction from their problems with love. I gradually realized that it didn't really matter to most people which party they worked for. Whether red or green or brown or black, the colors were almost as interchangeable as their shirts as long as the inner pain wasn't relieved. It's shocking when you consider the extent to which we are shaped by the spiritual wounds of the past. And we will not be able to create a positive renewal until we recognize the truth of this interrelation. It is really quite simple, since it's clearly visible for anyone who is prepared to look at it. But this is the point: We must be willing to look. As long as there is no hope of a positive solution or change, people will not show this willingness. As long as there is no land in sight, people will continue as they are. But if not we ourselves, who will deliver us from this eternal spell? Is everyone still waiting for the Messiah? No they aren't, and they seem to hate everyone who retains hope. Ulrich Horstmann, in his book The Monster, gives us some prophetic words which certainly contradict this attitude. He urges us to cherish life, safeguard love and provide children with a dependable and protective atmosphere in which to grow up. As long as there are people like this around, there is still hope of putting an end to primal pain. Since the trauma, which is contained in our horror films from the past, needs nourishment to survive, we can blot it out in a natural way by cutting off its fuel supply. This can be achieved by creating new human relations in which love is no longer punished and threatened with being cast away and forsaken.

The past is over. The continuation and revival of primal pain in adult relationships is a perpetual reproduction of the past. Whether or not the human race progresses or perishes doesn't depend on political or religious circumstances; it depends on whether or not the most aware and involved individuals are able to decipher and break through this vicious cycle within us. A renewal of love will only occur when it has been liberated from the unconscious trauma of the past and when we have succeeded in creating the structures of knowing love, through which the causes of the trauma can be removed. Therapy today is more than just the dissolution of these traumatic blockages; it involves developing new structures and new possibilities for love without fear and life without deception.

What is Jealousy and Where Does It Come From?

Out of the primal pain of being abandoned as a child there arises a psychological structure, which generally cannot be overcome as an adult. Every love relationship that we attempt in spite of this traumatic experience is internally linked to a fear of separation and abandonment. Love and fear of separation are intrinsically connected to one another. Out of this connection arises jealousy. In order to secure the relationship, both partners promise to be faithful, and then they watch over each other to make sure that the promise is kept. In the newspapers one always reads stories about the consequences of such commitments to be faithful. A young man in France shot his girlfriend. They fell in love five years ago and promised to never leave each other. When she did leave him, it was reason enough for him to kill her. I think it is quite easy to understand the thoughts and emotions that occurred here.

Jealousy, when it is genuine, behaves like a force of nature. It attacks the whole organism, fills it with fear and paralyzes it. Jealousy thus occurs as an organic phenomenon, which explains why it affects us so deeply. There is no doubt that it is a fundamental theme in the core area of our lives; it is to some extent the ABCs of the human organism. To spell love without jealousy means to spell life in a new way.

There is no sense in repressing or denying jealousy; it always arises when love and sex are concerned. Compared with the inner storm raging here, the ideas of free love often have very little power. You must keep in mind that while the storm of jealousy has existed for millennia, the concept of free love has only existed for a few years. So we don't want to make a brave last stand in an attempt to exterminate jealousy, for that would probably do away with love as well. Our task is to learn to recognize the patterns and forms of jealousy so that we can overcome it. We absolutely must achieve this in order to stop the suffering of generations of children who are forced to grow up in this culture of jealousy. There will be no peace on Earth until there is peace in love.

For everyone who has really been in love, women and men, jealousy has very understandable causes which directly affect us. We cannot bear to lose the good fortune that has been bestowed upon us. For an eighteen-year-old who has just discovered what intimate friendship with a girl means, this discovery is worth the whole world and he would sacrifice the whole world to keep it. Once he has gained possession of the treasure the drama begins. The need to guard and protect this treasure gives rise to a fear of losing it, which is the worst thing that could happen to him. So he clings to it even more tightly. The more he clings to her, the more justified his fears become because in so doing he suffocates their love and prevents it from growing. It's a vicious cycle right down to the bitter end, which usually consists of a dramatic separation, a cessation of all love impulses or an act of violence. How many tears have been shed because lovers believed they had to end a relationship out of a false feeling of injured pride, although they really didn't want to separate? How much potential bliss is contained in old letters which lie buried in dusty drawers?

Jealousy is the tragedy of our culture. Under such conditions, the fear of separation will continually find new nourishment. There are three reasons why a relationship in which you place all your hopes cannot be maintained. Firstly, both lovers thrust such an excessive amount of hope and expectation upon each other in the beginning that they are practically doomed to fail – no human being can fulfill such mammoth expectations. Secondly, because our society is built on the principles of profit and competition, and not according to the principles of love, lovers are forced to conform to the structures of society and must therefore internalize attitudes and behaviors that are hostile to love. Thirdly, it is due to the fact that love in our culture is based on many false assumptions, which inevitably cause love to disintegrate as long as we are unable to free ourselves from these assumptions. Foremost among these fatal concepts we find the division of the human world into couples. It is tantamount to the privatization and isolation of love within the bounds of two individuals under the exclusion of third parties, enforced by a disciplinary system in which any violation is punishable by jealousy and revenge.

Jealousy is certainly a very personal experience, but it is more than this. One could almost say that it is a deeply ingrained impulse which is derived from an ancient mythological image of love, as is marriage and the concept of marital devotion. This image, both in the development of the individual and the human race as a whole, originates in an infantile mythological layer of the soul which was formed under the miserable conditions of violence, fear and struggle for survival. For individuals, this concept is implanted in early childhood as a result of a family situation in which love is associated with the fear of being abandoned. In terms of the history of the human race, this concept was formed when the individual started separating itself from nature, which occurred simultaneously with the rise of civilization between 3000 and 1000 BCE. In both cases it meant a loss of security for the individual. The masculine and patriarchal mythology of love developed in this period as well, which includes such themes as buried treasure, dragon fights, eternal vows, lethal duels, damsels in distress, wedlock until death. Today we are easily able to comprehend these primordial images of our civilization, since we all carry them within us as archetypal remains. The psychological structures of the past are cemented inside of us like sedimentary rock.

Every epoch and every society has certain key principles which make up its spiritual backbone. It is these "paradigms" that decide over the fortune or misfortune of the society's members. The Judeo-Christian idea of a punishing god for example, produces a very real, concrete fear that still affects us on a cellular level even today, and which can be overcome neither by religious nor therapeutic means. Among these paradigms we must include the ancient myth of love and the belief that love and jealousy are inseparable. This idea is not only false; it is self-contradictory. Jealousy is not part of love – it is an obstacle to love. It is the death of love.

As long as the traditional sacrament of marriage remains so closely linked to such a narrow concept of fidelity, jealousy will continue to rage. No violent-free Earth, no sexpeace and no permanent love will be allowed to develop, neither on an individual basis between lovers, nor as a catalyst for an overall culture. In ecological, military and human terms, nothing has devastated our Earth more than the fatal guiding mechanism of this false concept of love. Nothing else has been more to blame for driving us to loneliness, despair, grief and cynicism. And nothing else has produced so many mental and physical diseases as the eternal waiting for fulfillment which is impossible under these circumstances. This should be included in the diagnosis of almost every psychosomatic illness: Patient is suffering from an incurable lovesickness caused by a false concept of love.

Concerning the theme "jealousy and rivalry," I would like to discuss an argument which comes up often in this context: Sexual rivalry was already present in animals. Stags, wolves, baboons and other animals fight for their preferred female with merciless savagery. In factual terms, it is certainly a sound and rational argument. But can this really serve as an argument for maintaining such a practice among humans? If our behavior were determined solely by the dictates of evolution, then there would be very little room left for further development. The evolution of our species is far from over. If we want to move forward, we cannot limit ourselves to the ideas of the past. In terms of evolution, the period of male rivalry is outdated. Today we are capable of using our cerebral capacities to create more humane structures.

If we have correctly understood the contemporary transformation processes of the collective subconscious, then we are allowed to say that we are now standing on the threshold of a new and fascinating historical era – the transition from the dream state to the waking state of consciousness, from mythological to knowing love, from the pedestal of marriage to the sacrament of free love. We can all give up jealousy without giving up love, if we really want to and if we know how.

These words may sound terse and over-simplified, but I still prefer not to add anything to them. There is no standard recipe. There is however a growing understanding of what I call "knowing love," an important part of which includes a mental grasp of the following section. The later chapter about fidelity should be understood in this context as well.

Is Asthma Part of Breathing?

Belief in jealousy seems to be confirmed by all the experiences of our daily existence. Jealousy is one of the most common motives for murder and evokes sympathy in any court of law. The whole world is steeped in rage. Extreme jealousy is regarded as a sign of true love. But still, seen from an adequate distance, it is an infantile phase of love which lasts so long only because people stop growing once this phase is reached. Before jealousy arose in the history of our spiritual development, love certainly took on different forms. And when jealousy finally disappears, we won't even be able to imagine that such a thing ever existed. That which was part of everyday life in one epoch can later appear as an unimaginable aberration of the past.

Is asthma part of breathing? Yes, under certain conditions. Otherwise the question would seem absurd. But it is not any more absurd than the question as to whether or not jealousy is part of love. Asthma isn't really part of breathing, but try to explain that to a nation of asthmatics! In light of the clear connection between air pollution and breathing difficulties, this example is not so farfetched. Let's assume that the whole human race has been suffering from asthma for millennia and cannot imagine life without it. Asthma and breathing are inseparable for them. They are only able to cure themselves of asthma by not breathing. But then of course they would die. So they believe that salvation is only possible in the hereafter.

Whoever claims that breathing is possible or even desirable without asthma is labeled a dreamer or an extremist. If others believe in him, they are called a sect. Anyone who performs in a vaudeville theater and presents a new method of breathing without asthma is marveled at or perhaps considered as a messiah. But if anyone seriously began to pave the way for a new society without asthma, they would be perceived as a threat to national security and singled out like Jonathan Livingston Seagull. Their friends would say they should at least look at the arguments of the other side; how can so many asthmatics be mistaken? If it turned into a large-scale movement, a general discussion would begin in the cities, on the campuses, in New Age groups, as to whether or not breathing is possible without asthma. And the most enlightened among them would say, "We should look at the issue empirically, not ideologically ... We have one-hundred-million asthmatics, two of them have occasional attacks of asthma-free breathing ... So we clearly have no evidence that breathing without asthma is possible (except perhaps under the influence of supernatural powers). We must therefore relegate this thesis to the realm of wishful thinking. We suspect that those who have proposed the theory are, due to untreated neurotic conditions, unable to lead a fulfilling and healthy life with asthma." The philosophers and priests of the asthmatic nation give their blessings to this scientific view as well. They raise their voice and tell us, "Asthma is as much part of breathing as the word is part of thought. The meaning of life is found in gratefully accepting and obeying the wise laws of creation." In this way, the asthmatics lived according to their principles for generations, until they finally perished from a lack of oxygen, just as the nation of the jealous before them had crumbled from a lack of love.

The Basic Contradiction of Love

Love has failed because of the inherent contradiction of form and content. Its form has been marriage, couple relationship and the exclusion of others. Its content, however, its natural and sexual energy, its source, its goal and its destiny cannot be restricted to any one person because it is dependent on communication, transmission and expansion. We have locked our happiness in a cage in order to preserve it, although the very purpose of this good fortune is to help us break out of cages. In this case too, it will either break out of its cage or it will wilt. Love between the genders, including couple relationships, need free love in order to grow. Couple love is not a private affair between two individuals; it is the entry into a new dimension of the world which brings with it a vital power of happiness and renewal. It may sound pompous, but it's true: Love between the genders is the beginning of a real human transformation. It is the transition from privacy and isolation to a more open general existence. The vows of marriage and all its consequences, however, cause just the opposite to occur: We privatize our happiness, retire to our cozy little paradise and try to seal it off from the outside. In this way, the power of transformation which is inherent in love has always been blocked. Love cannot reach its goal. Every generation must start at the beginning and will thus invariably run into the same contradiction until it is finally recognized and abolished. **Love that develops between two human beings must always go beyond them in order for it to retain its vital character.** This is true for sexual, spiritual and platonic love.

In his "Homage to Femininity" Teilhard de Chardin wrote a few lines which, because of their beauty and their innate truth, I cannot resist quoting here. The goddess everyone is searching for, be it Helen of Troy or the Fairy Queen in Nizami's tale, pronounces the following words:

"When a man loves a woman he thinks that his love is directed at an individual like himself whom he can incorporate into his sphere of influence and who desires to be united with him.

When he causes my face to glitter, he will discover a certain beam of light that sets his heart in motion and illuminates all things.

Soon however he is confused by the violent emotions that are unleashed within him as I draw near, and he senses that he cannot stay with me without inevitably becoming a servant of a universal work of creation.

He thought he had found a companion: but now he knows that in me he has touched upon a great hidden force, a mysterious and latent power which has approached him in this form in order to carry him away.

Whoever has discovered me stands upon the threshold of all things. When he realized how much I meant to him, he thought he could grasp me in his arms.

He wanted to lock himself up with me in a remote and isolated paradise where we would only need each other. It was at that moment that I vanished into thin air."

In order to comprehend the significance of these lines, it is necessary to read them over and over again. The woman speaking is a personification of love and she begins to dissolve in the moment the man attempts to possess her and lock her up in his private domain. In terms of its size and implications, love has become weighed down with so many absolute and infinite expectations that it is time to trim it back down to what it should be: a realization of intimacy and happiness between two human beings. Once we have found this source of expansion and entry into the world, our first reaction is to build a fence around it in order to monopolize it. This error has had such tormenting and fatal consequences that our language is at a loss to describe it. Love is free; it cannot be imprisoned. The most beautiful woman is also free; she cannot be privatized by a single man, regardless of his qualities. The privatization of love, as generally occurs in a conventional relationship or marriage, is equivalent to highway robbery – a plundering of the world. This is even suggested by the etymology of the word "private": like the word "deprive," it comes from the Latin verb "privare," meaning "to rob."

We must be prepared to recognize and accept this in order to understand the latent violence that is present in every relationship. There can be no peace on Earth before there is peace in love. No more can be said with words.

PART IV:

LIBERATING EROS

A Universal Process of Emerging Love

The destiny of unfulfilled love is an individual destiny, but our world is made up of the sum of these individual destinies. To put it mildly, our world is suffering from a severe case of lovesickness. Cosmetic repairs can no longer help the situation, and neither can the most solemn vows. The only thing that can help us now is new knowledge and insight; its effect must reach all the way into our cells. The world and we need a new recipe for love. So many of us have perished from its savage consequences that it can no longer be kept private. The question of love is central to a new order of life on our planet. All forms of sensual love, including homosexuality, must be allowed to develop freely without fear, so that all members of the human race can come together and integrate in a new way. Only then can a concrete solution be found for the problems which are causing our lives to fall apart worldwide.

The atrocities, errors and complications of our history have for the most part been a consequence of the hopelessness of Eros. All political and intellectual revolutions have avoided this subject. This despair has been a result of false information. Human behavior has been guided for millennia by images and ideas that do not correspond to the essence of Eros. The myth of marriage, the dogma of restricting love to two people, the axiom of jealousy – in the midst of this flood of misinformation it was not possible to establish peace between the genders, nor a real home for children, nor love for the rest of creation.

The world has entered an apocalyptic phase. The old systems are bursting; the traditional dogmas have lost their influence; the rotten crust has been peeled off "to make way for new life to blossom in the ruins." The world is "ripe" for rebirth.

These painful and often unsuccessful attempts to release love from its imprisonment have put a universal process into motion which affects all of us. We are twisting and writhing like a woman about to give birth. There is no way back; our old dreams are all dried out. It is no longer a question of personal taste; it is an objective historical transformation.

Of course we are the ones who are responsible for this transformation, not some abstract or divine being. It will only depend on us how far it goes and if it happens at the right time. But if it happens, it won't only affect the individual; it will affect the organism of the human race as a whole, because we are all linked to this organism by what one could call "morphogenetic fields" – the changing information of the genetic code. The universal consciousness adjusts automatically when new information arises which is pertinent to the core areas of our existence. This information is then recorded in the "code" of love. According to Victor Hugo, "Nothing is more powerful than an idea whose time has come." The power of this new information will not be visible at once. It is similar to the power of a sprouting plant which breaks through an asphalt surface. It is the power of an individual in the process of becoming and it is in resonance with the becoming of the world. That is why resonance is the code name for freed love.

We shouldn't always have to fight alone for the liberation of sensual love. Love prefers to nest in places where the struggle is already over. The only thing we really have to fight against is our own habits, fallacies and illusions. The most important thing is that we see and understand the goal, and that we genuinely desire to reach it. Not even God can help those who don't truly want to reach the goal. Some would rather die than face the truth of these new ideas. But then that's their own business. When new will power arises as a result of new insight and recognition, our own capabilities become linked to higher forces. In other words, an individual process comes into harmony with a universal process, which is what gives us the inspiration and the strength to continue. Eros is not merely an individual force; it is also a cosmic one. The linking of our experience of sexuality and love to this universal process strengthens our determination to succeed. Even our own identity expands beyond that which our own individual power would otherwise allow. We become immune to the prejudices of others and waste no energy discussing things that no longer need to be discussed. Once we have sensed where the source lies, there is nothing that can keep us from searching for it.

The most fulfilling achievement of love is the reunification of our divided world. It was divided between humankind and the rest of creation from which we originate. We stand out so much because of our inner desolation, the fear of being abandoned and the pain of lost love. The harder we try to hold onto love, the more rapidly it flees from us, since there is nothing that can contain the object of our desire. When the human being finally breaks through all the barriers after a long period of abandonment then he returns into the presence of a greater world. He senses his arrival and experiences it as love. Love means arrival – woman with man, man with woman, the human being with himself and heaven within the human being. All of life waits for this moment.

A Culture Free of Sexual Repression

The suppression of sexuality has always been a fundamental pillar of society. It has become so widespread and so deeply ingrained that it no longer occurs consciously, but rather in the form of an unconscious reflex. That is why we are often no longer aware of it as such; the repressed sexual content is not even perceived by the conscious mind. Only with the aid of trained self-observation can we detect the impulses which take only a fraction of a second to flash through body and mind. They are often wonderfully erotic and energetic images, which immediately clash with the so-called principles of human dignity and are thus repressed. The images are repressed and the energies are blocked, both in the form of an involuntary counter-reaction which is likewise completed within a fraction of a second.

We can test this in an interesting self-awareness experiment: let's try to hold back the repression of the sexual impulse instead of the impulse itself. This means restoring the organism to its natural state of sexual desire and arousal – turning it over to its own energetic impulses and images. What an incredibly high voltage immediately begins to fill our whole existence. Imagine all the sources of insight and knowledge that lie before us! A whole series of wonderful discoveries could begin as long as the pain of these new joys isn't too great. A discovery in bed for example: pressing and squeezing, extending and stretching, movements that used to cause pain now give rise to the most arousing stimulations. The fact that the body can be freed from pain so easily is proof that this condition is brought about by unconscious repressive processes. One may also discover a completely new lightness and power of motion when the inner will no longer operates against sexual energies, but instead is unified with them. Just imagine the level of communication and erotic energy that could be released! The secret of vitality consists of developing an inner strength, which could do away with all of our troubles and self-pity if we only gave it a chance. The secret of our culture consists of responding to this force with the internalized and automatic mechanism of repression. This was the incomprehensible discovery of Wilhelm Reich, which was much sharper and much larger in scope than Sigmund Freud's theories.

This truth holds the key to a radically new civilization; whoever is capable of recognizing it is faced with one of the most devastating facts that a knowing consciousness will ever encounter. Imagine all the knowledge about life and human existence that we would have access to if repression didn't exist.

Think of everything that has been conjured up in the name of exalted humanity and culture only because repression was faster than the intellect and because the mind's eye was prevented from seeing what it is inside of us that holds this world together.

In the course of human history there may never have existed a time in which we took responsibility for our earthly actions without blaming part of it on supernatural powers. In order to develop an erotic culture without repression we need a transformation which would enable us to once again accept the responsibility for our actions that we have up to now attributed to gods, spirits, stars or simply destiny. This includes accepting responsibility for apparently self-evident truths such as tradition and morality. In the wake of Nietzsche's words "God is dead" we are finally able to grasp the extent of this historical transformation. Structures, which have evolved more or less unconsciously, such as government, economy, family, social and moral order and religion must now be examined and reshaped by human beings who are becoming increasingly autonomous. The transformation of sexuality is part of this process as well. In order to promote health, the doctor Wilhelm Reich called for the dissolution of all forms of sexual suppression and repression. Whether or not we follow his advice is no longer a matter of taste or intellectual preference; it is a matter of knowledge and common sense. So much pseudo-culture, philosophic insanity and human cruelty have resulted from unlived sexuality that no knowledgeable person can escape the following statement: the possibility for a humane culture only exists once the sexual repression and coercion of it have been eliminated.

The ending of sexual repression can neither be instituted by decree, nor can it be brought about through violence or revolution.

It is an internal process that everyone must decide on for themselves. However, we can create networks and meeting places among ourselves which gradually take on a larger scale and which encourage sexual liberation, because there is no longer any reason to continue the traditional double morality. This book should provide a powerful impulse in that direction. Now it's time for action.

Knowing Love

The liberation of love is linked to a process of recognition and insight, which in this book is called knowing love. This is a fact which needs to be emphasized, for it runs contrary to the ideas we generally have about love. Most people regard love and sex as a matter of feeling and emotion, not as a matter of the mind. They say, "My mind might agree with your ideas, but my gut does not." They are mistaken. Their gut would certainly agree to these ideas if their minds didn't put up such resistance. It is the mind that refuses to let go of jealousy; it is in the mind that ideas of revenge are produced after the failure of a relationship; it is the mind that persistently refuses to accept the ideas of free love and to recognize its truth and naturalness. We all know intuitively, in our cells as it were, that these ideas are true, but the adversary is in the mind. The mind has its reasons for not wanting liberation, even if the body desires nothing but release. It is in the mind that the disastrous calculations are made, resulting in new possibilities being rejected.

These calculations are usually very transparent and simple; they go something like this: "The ideas are fine, but what would my boyfriend, girlfriend, partner say?" "I'm completely convinced of these ideas, but my husband is terribly jealous." "My wife and I have created a common destiny for ourselves; I can't put that at stake just because of truth in love." "I know that my love life is nothing but one big lie, but I need this lie to keep the peace at home." Thus the truth is not in conflict with the desires or the feelings that people have, but with the systems that they have hammered into their minds in order to survive in the face of a hopeless life situation.

Once you have come to understand the biographical and emotional backgrounds behind such structures of untruth in the love life of human beings there is little inclination to make any moral judgments; you understand why the majority of people have chosen such a strange way of life and why they do not want to reconsider. Those, however, who are not yet so firmly entangled in the snares of their closed systems are in a position to help develop the potential of knowing love.

As long as love remains a merely emotional process it will not last. As quickly as you emotionally fall in love, you will fall out of love again; as emotionally as you love one person on one day, you might love another on the next day. Of course both partners know this instinctively, and thus they will react to this secret knowledge with rage and jealousy at the emotional level. Once the emotions have created a dynamic of their own, called passion, reason no longer stands a chance. Passion is a storm in the heart and body without pause, without reflection, without questioning. It is always the beginning of the end, a wonderfully beautiful theme for operas and operettas, and a terribly destructive force for real people. The depth and sensual pleasure of knowing love is more than passion: it is passion plus knowledge plus reflection. It is passion which has been deepened, purified and pacified in the realms of the mind. It is like a lake whose bottom becomes visible even at great depth because the storms have calmed down. You can see into the depths and discern what is there.

Love, which has gone beyond mere emotion and passion, does not blind you; it makes you see. It is the foremost element in life which brings awakening and knowledge. The fact that sexuality and knowledge are linguistically identical in ancient Hebrew makes deep sense (as in the symbol of the 'tree of knowledge' or in the phrase, 'Adam knew his wife'). Today this identity is beginning to reappear in the first experiences of knowing love. For centuries love and sexuality have been the victims of lies and repression to the extent that it became impossible to understand this innermost equation in our lives, the identity between sensual love and knowledge. Now that we are rediscovering it, our path toward knowledge is being given a new meaning and a new direction. It could well be the beginning of a new era.

Love sometimes makes you see, even though you might not really want to. In the childish manner of hearts that are in love, both sexual and emotional love tends to avoid insight as long as possible. If love wants to survive however, it will eventually be forced to gain insight. You may come to realize, for example, that you can find all those things that you feared your partner might secretly be thinking in your own mind too, so there is no point in condemning them in the other. You may come to understand that clinging to your partner will result in love being suffocated and that it is therefore quite useless to attempt to save the relationship in this way. You may realize that your own jealousy will last until you overcome certain intellectual or sexual difficulties and insincerities. You may learn that love can only grow on the basis of trust, and trust in turn only on the basis of truth. What grows on the basis of untruth is obsession and has nothing to do with love. You may also realize that there is no point in trying to childishly blackmail love and sex from a person.

When we have finally gained these insights, we are amazed and shocked at everything we have done so far. We are bewildered at what we ourselves are capable of doing, while constantly suspecting others and putting the blame on them. Couple relationships in our culture seem to be based on a system of mutual reproach; between more "reasonable" partners this is not performed as an open dispute anymore, but in a more subtle, non-verbal way. Migraine headaches, breathing problems, anorexia or obesity are used. Today continual silence has taken the place of arguing and bickering. Since this is also hard to cope with in the long run, there are occasional clarifying discussions, workshops on relationship issues, group discussions and other edifying activities to keep things going.

In knowing love, attention is no longer focused only on oneself, but increasingly on the partner. It is not along the lines of jealousy and latent reproaches, nor is it in order to obtain ammunition for the next battle. The goal is to start discovering our partner anew, to notice that we have not really known each other, that we have not really wanted to truly know each other yet. We have not even been aware of the fact that we do not know each other yet and we have so far lived next to, but not with each other. We know how much sugar the other takes with their coffee; and we can tell by the expression on our partner's face that it might be better to just keep some distance for a while. We learn to be diplomatic and considerate with each other and believe we know each other until one day we are amazed and bewildered at things we would never have even suspected. Our parents have shared their lives with each other, have lain side by side every night. But have they known each other? And when one of them passed away, did the other know who the person had really been who had just died? The marriage was mostly like a thick and familiar layer of daily details, covering up the reality underneath.

In knowing love you start seeing your partner in a new way and you also start seeing love in a new way. It is often linked to a feeling of great love and sometimes also of equally great remorse. There is so much that you have missed, neglected, misunderstood and judged too hastily in your everyday blindness. All the detours and tortures that could have been avoided if only one had been able to truly see at the right time. It is so much that there is no point in reacting sentimentally or reproaching yourself now. These are no longer the tears of the opera that you are crying now, but the tears of insight, if there are any tears at all. All you desire at this point is to right the wrong that you have done to yourself; you deeply hope that it is not too late. Knowing love is a new beginning. What I wish for myself and all those who love is that we do not destroy this beginning by falling back into our old habits.

Trust as a Recipe for Healing

Fear is the breeding place for violence; trust is the breeding place for love. The history of civilization up to now, which we have constructed in the name of morality, religion and social order has been a history of structural violence based on fear. It is fear that is responsible for contracting our cells, closing our minds and tying up our bodies. It is fear that turns the gift of love into a muddle of torment and confusion. It is the same fear that leads us to counter the issue of sexuality with morality and pedantry, instead of with candor and truth. Fear is a virus that destroys love and afflicts the body with disease, for "fear devours the soul."

The power required to overcome fear is the power of trust. It is the healing power of life itself. If we have trust, we require no further educational or therapeutic measures, since the old wounds heal naturally in an environment of trust. The main idea of this book, which is inherently connected to the theme of free love, consists of replacing our living conditions of structural violence with conditions of structural trust. The ideas of free love are meaningless without trust because they would thus be deprived of their basis. Free love is only possible where Eros is linked to trust. Where this is not the case, all that can result from the idea of free love is a shallow ideology, a cult or a mere antithesis to conventional love relationships.

Trust is not a moral, but a biological category, which is why it immediately begins to cure disrupted bodily processes. The age-old wounds of fear, psychosomatic contractures, energy congestion and infections can often be completely eliminated through a single experience of trust (a relapse is possible if the situation reverses).

Long-lasting trust between human beings cannot be established by moral or religious commandments; it can only occur if we treat each other in an honest and truthful way, especially in the more intimate areas where lies and deceit have evolved into a sort of life diplomacy. Acting honestly in the areas of sex and love could offer a means of cultural renewal to help cure us of this disease that we are all suffering from. We shouldn't rely so heavily on ideas borrowed from other cultures and religions to solve problems which are so important for our own spiritual renewal. We don't need anything more than our own mind and will power. We can occupy ourselves with Indian cultures as long as we keep in mind that trust is to a large extent a sexual issue in our culture. We can certainly learn about Tibetan and Taoist wisdom, but we must remember that solutions to the problem of trust cannot be found in Nirvana, but have to be worked out in concrete interaction between human beings. We can eat health foods or maintain a macrobiotic diet, but we must not forget that the bread of love tastes much different. We can continue to listen to the voices of the wise, but we must not overlook the fact that the truth and beauty of love can only be attained if we follow the voice of our own body, our own heart and our own mind. All the approaches of the New Age movement may be meaningful in one way or another, as long as they don't add to suppression. But the genuine transformation and redemption of our lives will only occur when we witness the coming together of Eros and trust, sex and truth, sensuality and friendship. Once we no longer have to shield ourselves from one another, we can move forward together and generate so much momentum that trust will be instilled in others as well.

An Alternative Concept of Faithfulness

I have said quite a lot about the much too narrow concept of fidelity in this book. But the question of being faithful must also be examined for its own sake, at least in a very brief but intensive manner. As has been shown in previous sections of this book, fidelity is diametrically opposed to love. The liberation of Eros cannot succeed until we have wiped out every trace of the old idea of fidelity, which is based on the principle of the exclusion of others. Faithfulness has nothing to do with a ban, with a vow or with a contract. It is a concrete love relationship between two human beings. I am faithful to him because I love him. My love cannot depend on the condition that he should not go to bed with anyone else. If my partner is an attractive human specimen then it is normal that others should desire him and that he should desire others. He feels exactly the same way about it as I do. Should we really be expected to show our loyalty and devotion by renouncing such pleasures for the sake of another? What sort of farcical, masochistic idea is that? Faithfulness is love, but love is not renunciation. If our devotion for one another falls apart as a result of other sexual contacts, then our love was built on sand. What petty and trifling thoughts generate such a concept of fidelity – and how narrow these partners of love must view their relationship in order to place such burdens on one another! Show me that you love me by promising me that you will give up that which is dearest to you, all of your other sexual contacts! Hold that in front of the mind's eye. It is really no wonder that we have failed as of yet to create an erotic and loving civilization.

So what is fidelity then, really? It means being there for those we love. To be faithful is to show warm friendship and concrete solidarity. It has to do with trust. There is trust between us because we know that we don't lie to each other. We cannot be turned against each other through spreading false rumors because each of us knows what the other does and what he doesn't do. A precondition for fidelity is that we know one another. If we still love each other once we have gotten to know each other then we can say that we are faithful to one another. We remain faithful even when our partner commits flagrant violations because we know that he has reasons for what he does, although they may be false. We criticize each other, but we always seek forgiveness once the misunderstanding has been cleared up. The relationship we have to one another is not legally binding and is not tainted with feelings of revenge or resentment. Faithfulness develops over a long period of time and embodies a feeling of love and absolute unity. But it is still an active expression of will and an active affirmation of the partner: I want to lead a common life with this person; I don't want to lie to him; I want to support him and help him to develop as best I can. I want to recognize and overcome my faults and carelessness together with him and I want to have a sexual relationship with him as long as it doesn't degenerate into daily routine. At the same time I want to make sure that there is sufficient tension and occasional distance in our relationship so that we can approach each other anew every time we meet. I want to make the most important decisions in my life together with him, and my innermost feelings reassure me that we will never part.

These are the words of faithfulness spoken from the viewpoint of free love. Our parents and grandparents would have gladly spoken about each other in this way, but they couldn't because their capacity for love was crippled by their obedience to the law of sexual exclusiveness. When some of them grew old together and lived happily ever after, it was despite their mistaken vow of fidelity, and not because of it. Faithfulness as it is described above generally develops between two individuals, but it cannot be restricted to just two. It provides us with a model that can be used to build similar intimate relationships with all people we love. The love between my life companion and myself has long served as a prototype for all other relationships that are important to me. The obsolete vow of fidelity, in which two people promise to restrict sexuality to only one another, is a frontal attack against one of the most remarkable and meaningful laws of love: its innate tendency to spread out from its focal point in all directions.

Sometimes fidelity in the old sense can be helpful at the beginning of a relationship in order to protect it and stabilize it. But the fence must be removed when it is stable enough. We can only remain faithful over a long period of time if we are allowed to love others as well. It is this revelation that has laid the foundations for the gentle revolution of knowing love.

De-psychologizing Love

Earlier generations were not able to deal with the issue of Eros; they simply ignored it. In recent times this habit has been replaced by a different procedure: now we prefer to carry on endless discussions about sexuality, love and partnership. The same arguments and the same mistakes are repeated over and over again in these "rational" discussions. Because of the difficulty of this type of debate, the issue becomes all bogged down with psychological matters; it becomes "psychologized" or "rationalized." Unfortunately, this is a step in the wrong direction; we should be attempting instead to rescue love from the grips of psychology and reason.

Our bodies have become so weighed down by psychological considerations that they are no longer able to breathe freely. Our heads as well are so inundated with psychological slogans that we can no longer think and see clearly. The most important prerequisite for the liberation of body, mind and heart may be to reduce the "intellectualization" of our behavior and environment.

Both our inner and outer surroundings have become muddled as a result of so much mental masturbation. The more you let the problems get to you and the more you try to deal with them rationally, the more blurred the issue becomes and the deeper it gets lost in the fog. Real love however makes us see clearly.

Our personal thoughts and feelings are so distant from all great events; our everyday toils are so removed from true fulfillment. When IT finally arrives, our mind will be in no position to receive it.

Those who are concerned with matters of sex and love activate many attitudes and feelings in others, since they usually have similar problems and find themselves in the same apparently hopeless situation. And because so many problems are discussed and formulated, we continually feel obliged to deal with them. We thereby miss the opportunity of having new experiences and thus block the entry of Eros into our lives. Under these circumstances it isn't really such a bad idea to leave our cliques behind and search on our own.

I would like to remind you of the parable of the elephant (see page 105). The more the elephant broods over ways of freeing his leg, the more difficult it becomes. Without realizing it, he only makes his situation worse because in reality he is not focusing his thoughts on his freedom, but on his chains. In the end, all the efforts that were actually intended to release him from his affliction only added to his suffering. He rationalizes his situation and tries to solve his problem with an intellect that is in a very bad state, instead of using a fresh and clear perspective.

The problems we have do not make up an intrinsic part of our nature; we have merely unwittingly identified ourselves with them and adopted them. We talk very personally about ourselves when we are actually referring to our personal histories. The result is that we fail to realize the extent to which we are capable of solving many of our problems on our own. Our "soul" is not just the sum of our mental and intellectual capacities; it is the inner space that fills up at sublime and exalted moments. The soul, which has disintegrated into thousands of reactions of stimulus and response, must be brought together again so that we can find its center. When this is accomplished, the soul will no longer be characterized by a confusion of feelings; it will become an expression of higher sensation. We all have an idea of what is meant here. Once we have escaped from the throngs of daily life and entered the zones of inner silence, serene reflection and perhaps even love, the world appears to us for a moment as a strange yet familiar sight. At this point of contact we have the impression, though only for a few brief seconds, that the coordinates of our universe become brighter and more transparent and that our sense of perception is intensified, because something within us is filled with expectation, surprise and gratitude.

These are the true emanations of the soul, the language of the source, which we should once again begin to understand and cultivate in order to get back "on track" after being led astray for so long. The right track is still the mystery and the elemental shock we call "love."

Such experiences generally only last for a few seconds before they are overshadowed by the clouds of everyday life. To turn these fleeting moments into a permanent state, which is the goal of our journey, we need new venues for communication without pretense, truth without denunciation and sexual desire without fear of contempt. Eros has the power to free body and mind from their psychological and intellectual clutches. But in order to bring this about, we must first understand its laws. Eros will come forth by itself once we have paved the way for it.

Creating Spaces for a New Encounter of the Genders

In order to further develop the possibilities of Eros, we need concrete opportunities for actions, experiences and perspectives. The unleashing of Eros will only be achieved if there are people who make a conscious and active effort to bring it about. Attempts such as partner swapping and houses for tolerant couples deserve to be praised, but they are no solution because they are simply too limited in their scope and are generally restricted to a controlled and oversimplified program. Experiments in free sexuality, carried out by the Austrian artist Otto Muehl in Burgenland or by the Sannyasin founder Bhagwan Shree Rajneesh in Puna, India, showed more meaningful prospects, because they were integrated in new living conditions. Yet still, they were too strongly linked to membership in a certain group or belief system. Despite their failure, they have set a development in motion that we cannot ignore. We need venues, meeting places and networks where free encounters between lovers and seekers are possible without the usual suppression, pretense, double standards and sexual frustration. We need places where women and men can occasionally fill up their tanks with sex when they are dying of thirst. We need meeting places of a new sort, where both genders can go on the most stimulating research trip that exists in this universe: the exploration of sensual love with all its sexual and spiritual surprises, pleasures and revelations. Preferably for all age groups, since sexual hunger and the desire for love are not restricted to any particular age.

After having thought about what the opportunity really means, many people would offer buildings or property for such a project. Perhaps some of you who read this book have the energy to realize a full-scale project like this. Venues of all kinds would be suitable, e.g. conference halls, resorts, lakeshore properties, hotels or other buildings with generous green space, cruise ships, islands, etc.

A meeting place for free love similar to that described in this book could be set up, not too commercial, accessible to everyone, with no ideological slant, but lively, imaginative and effervescent

– a real attraction. There would be cafés, bars and other meeting places; there would be a beach, nature and beautiful landscapes; and somewhere there would be an Eros academy, a research center dealing with questions of sensual love. There may even be a sort of "brothel" which, upon closer examination, would reveal quite different characteristics. Sexuality would be practiced here, not for money, but for reasons of lust, beauty and necessity. Here people could do what they would be doing anyway if they weren't prevented from doing it by our antiquated morality, but in this case without humiliation and violence.

Such a project would of course be accessible to both genders. Women would be "served" in the same way as men, as long as it arises naturally and there is no obligation. So that it all runs smoothly, some of the more mature women may need to give advice and oversee things a bit. The temple priestess of ancient cultures could have a very central function in such a project. And in general I think women should assume the leading roles here so that sensual love remains the focus, and not money and power, as is the case in patriarchal institutions. But this is only meant as a piece of advice; I don't want to deter anyone from participating who has something to contribute. Regardless of whether it comes from women or men, what we need most for these projects is initiative and synergy.

In order to get a more vivid picture of what life could be like there and what it all means, I want to quote a few passages from the book Rettet den Sex [Save Sexuality] by Sabine Lichtenfels in which a similar Eros project is described as science fiction:

> "The biggest advantage of the Garden of Delights is that all those who go there discover that they desire sexual contact, or at least that they are not averse to the idea. This gives rise to an unusually light and relaxed atmosphere where, for example, one might ask another: 'Can I fulfill any of your wishes?' The other knows immediately what was meant and replies, depending on the situation and the degree of attraction, 'Yes, of course' or, 'Thank you for asking, but at the moment I'm looking for someone else.' Then they continue on their way and perhaps address the

next attractive passerby, if they feel like it. The inhabitants of the Garden of Delights, the reborn, are surprisingly uncomplicated in this matter.

Somehow there is always a sense of anticipation since everyone knows that they will get what they desire. You might say that they are all well taken care of. They are all sure that they will find sexual satisfaction and therefore are not in such a hurry. These encounters are not burdened with psychological tension and pressure, as used to be the case. You could meet in the tavern or in the Japanese tea-room and chat about Zen Buddhism or anthroposophy. Even during the most interesting conversations it isn't necessary to conceal your enthusiasm for the voluptuousness of your partner. Nervous sexual vibrations no longer represent an obstacle to conversation and the exchange of ideas. On the contrary, the synchronization of their thoughts heightens their sensual anticipation, which in turn increases the intensity of their conversation. How distracted we used to be as a result of our unfulfilled desire! When a man had a woman in front of him and spoke with her about everything under the sun, his inner eye was always focused on her breasts or on her behind, on everything that was hidden beneath her dress. The mind and the words were not in the same place. How easy it is now to fulfill and enjoy both of these poles of life – the spiritual and the sensual! These two forces were never really opposed to each other; we finally see how easy it is to unite them …

It is interesting to observe what sort of sexual partners are sought out and chosen by what sort of people. It is for example intriguing to see how young men approach older, more mature women and how these experienced women enjoy making love to them and initiating them. Age differences suddenly take on a positive and sensual quality …

It is surprising, but actually not really surprising, how quickly newcomers find their way around and the ease with which they utilize the existing possibilities; how seventeen-year-old girls derive pleasure and confidence from their experiences, and how they are able to approach desired partners with no trouble, despite their bashfulness. There are no reproachful or cynical thoughts that you have to protect yourself from, neither before nor after. In this place there is practically no condemnation or castigation at all. The system works according to a natural principle of direct human feedback and understanding.

It is also interesting to look at the medical development taking place in the Garden. Women and men who are already wilting begin to blossom out; their bodies recover and become round or firm, depending on individual temperament. It is the voluptuous pleasure and sexual fulfillment that bring about this process of healing which has surpassed all previous therapeutic achievements. But this doesn't surprise anybody. It is no secret that a fifty-year-old or even seventy-year-old woman can flourish again through the reactivation and renewed fulfillment of her sensual existence. It is natural that a seventeen-year-old boy will thrive if he has the opportunity to be with a more mature woman with whom he can realize his sexual fantasies. A process of healing is automatically set in motion, whereby the astonishing thing is that what we instinctively and unconsciously sense to be true does in fact become reality. Essentially, it is nothing more than the plain and simple rediscovery of how to savor and enjoy life."

The sixteen-year-old Sonja asked me if she was allowed to go there. Of course she can; there is no age restriction. Young people need meeting places where they can learn about sensual love under the protection and assistance of others who have more experience, but where they are not simply told what to do. It is especially important that they gain such experience before they have bound themselves to the role models provided for them by their parents or other adults.

A free but responsible school of love for young people! There are many international youth centers and meeting places, but you will hardly find one where such issues are openly and properly discussed, together with concrete opportunities to experience them. During the day they participate in sports, group meetings and discussions about spiritual and intellectual matters, and at night they lie in bed with blood boiling in their veins and think about completely different things. This would be a real opportunity to correct the course of inner human development.

But a center for free love concerns all ages, not just young people. The sexual issue often intensifies at an age where normal social conditions offer little or no possibility for the realization of such contacts. Let's look at women over 40 again. They are still young and have usually been through a marriage and several unsuccessful relationships. In theory, they should be free for a new beginning. Their sexuality is in full bloom, but they lack the opportunity to take advantage of it without remorse. How can a society claim that it functions according to humane principles when one-forth of its population is forced to live without sexuality at the height of their lives? If we are so thoughtful as to organize a "ball for lonely hearts," then why can't we go just a little bit further and create larger centers which are open to all, regardless of whether their hearts are lonely or not, regardless of whether they are looking for a partner for life or for a few exciting hours.

As we have seen, neither marriage nor brothel is a solution to the sexual problems facing us. There are many couples that don't want to split up even though their marriages are over, either because of children or because they once loved each other. They could go to this place and rediscover how to enjoy life. By opening a new channel toward the outside, they could find a new channel to each other as well. They do not need to decide for or against their marriage, but they gain a new basis of experience that could help them to understand and reinvigorate their friendship. Many lovers break up simply because they see no other alternative. If they saw an alternative, they would not be so burdened by worry and indecision and could allow themselves time to resolve their quarrel. Hardly anyone disputes the fact that the establishment of such projects for the liberation of love would correspond to the secret wishes of a countless number of men and women. It would be the project of the century! Once word gets around that it's serious and that it's not another commercial gimmick, get ready for a mass migration. On a South Pacific island or another chosen place there will arise a mecca of love, the realization of an age-old dream, but with the definitive will to solve the issue of sensual love in our time. Pilot projects for a new sexual humanism are only the beginning.

Sexpeace and Greenpeace: Peace between the Genders and Peace with Nature

The ecological disaster and the sexual disaster are interconnected. The destruction of the life energies in the human organism and the destruction of the life energies in our biosphere are two aspects of the same basic problem. Sexpeace and Greenpeace – the healing of our sexual nature and the healing of the biosphere's ecological nature – are therefore two crucial aspects of the global task we are facing today. This very briefly is the main point which will be elaborated in more detail in this chapter.

The Earth is not a motor which runs smoothly if only the right kind of oil and gas are provided. Neither does it get sick only because it is being polluted by industrial wastewater, acid rain, carbon dioxide and other kinds of toxins. Its illness encompasses much more than just its mechanical malfunctioning, because its inner core, its soul, has been affected. Our biosphere is a most diverse and yet homogeneous organism, where body and soul interact very much in the same way as they do in the organism of the individual. Based on what we know today, and on an honest synopsis of all recent findings, we cannot doubt the fact that our planet must be viewed in such a holistic way and that a soul exists in all life processes. We can clearly relegate the question of whether other living beings have a soul to the past. The discovery of a unified connectedness of all life is part of the fundamental development currently taking place in enlightened religion and science. For the most part our current ecology is still too closely oriented toward the old mechanistic worldview. It usually overlooks the spiritual aspect of the world and therefore reaches false or incomplete conclusions. Although the separation of the two terms is inappropriate, healing ecology is defined as the healing of both spiritual and biological processes in the overall organism of the biosphere.

Life in our own organism and life in the biosphere around us is made up of the same energy: universal life energy. In the course of being discovered it has received many names, such as Chi, Mana,

Prana, Orgone, etc. Many different aspects of it have been described, but rarely its sexual aspect (except in Wilhelm Reich's work). Sexual energy, however, is one of the main aspects of universal life energy within any organism. Universal life energy appears in various states of matter, either more solidified or more refined. It affects everything that has to do with our sexuality as well as our emotions and thoughts, and plays a decisive role in determining whether we are ill or in good health. It affects all outer processes of growth and creation, overall natural circulatory systems and even the weather. It forms the psychological as well as the meteorological atmosphere. Spontaneous changes in the weather, which coincide with intense psychological events, are based on this interconnection. The entire biosphere possesses a unified energy system, a unified system of information stored in the genetic code, and a unified system of matter consisting of chemical elements and their properties. In addition it can apparently withstand an enormous amount of strain and, due to its inherent self-healing power, can regenerate itself with nearly inexhaustible power. Otherwise there would no longer be any sprouting, blossoming, singing or laughing, after all that we have inflicted upon it for millennia. On the one hand we are facing outer destruction, consisting of the extermination of large populations and species, the pollution of the air and the contamination of the water, the breeding of fur-bearing animals and livestock, the hunting of whales and the killing of seals. On the other hand we are facing destruction from within, consisting of a lack of meaning and purpose in life, the fear of life itself, the loss of the ability to love, and psychosomatic illnesses of various kinds. Together they exert such a great amount of strain on the global organism that it is only a matter of time before it snaps. The crises in our inner and outer environments are two sides of the same problem and can be understood and solved only by adopting an overall view.

When we consider the amount of violence against children, native peoples and animals occurring on a global scale, it is obvious that a new concept of human civilization is necessary. The innermost core of this concept touches the most elemental and basic human questions concerning sexuality, love and partnership, community and belonging, the meaning of life and home. Whether a future society remains inhuman or whether it can become humane, whether children growing up will be happy or unhappy in their society, will to a great extent depend on how we approach and solve our inner questions. This is the reason these inner questions are currently our main historic issues, and at their very center we find the most bitter paradox of our times: Why, in our cultural environment, are far more people suffering and dying from unsolved problems of sexuality and love than from all other illnesses of civilization? We have not only ruined the Earth, but because we have continually neglected and even attacked our own sexual, emotional and mental energy, we have ruined ourselves as well. Even the Pepsodent smiles can no longer gloss over this fact.

"Thou shalt subdue the Earth!" This biblical phrase has determined the fate of the Earth like no other. We have in deed made the gigantic attempt at subduing the Earth, and have turned against the Earth and its nature by using mechanical intelligence and brutal technology directed at overcoming resistances instead of seeking resonance. This has resulted in methods of exploitation, suppression and domination by force which we have utilized not only against our own kind, but also against all our fellow creatures and creation as a whole. We have not subdued the Earth through tender nursing and cultivation or through positive guidance, but by means of outright destruction. The technologies used so far have been technologies of domination aimed at overcoming resistances instead of cooperating with the energies and life forces of creation. This resistance-oriented attitude has determined how children are raised, how young people are educated, how animals are kept, how forests are chopped down, how rivers are straightened, how war is waged and how whole nations are annihilated. This attitude has resulted in a structurally violent relationship toward ourselves and toward the world. We have bypassed the natural laws of the biosphere with its ecological cycles, its spherical intricacies, its living emanations, and its spiritual network made up of myriads of creatures. We have replaced all of this with the power of violence.

We have created scientific, moral and religious systems which are opposed to the way in which all of life, universal energy and Eros function. Whenever a neglected child has to find new and crooked paths in order to receive love and attention, and (s)he instead reaps either moral or physical punishment, structural violence is created. Whenever his/her curiosity and desire to play is suppressed by the one-dimensional rationalism of adults, structural violence is created. Whenever sexuality and love are forced into narrow rules and codes, into a too narrow monogamous relationship or into a strict promise to be faithful forever, structural violence is created. Whenever an authentic religious experience that a person may have is imprisoned into the dogma of a church, structural violence is created.

All dogmas and all structures that are too rigid are dams which hold back life. Any attempt at leveling life or forcing it into too narrow channels creates a subliminal reservoir of destruction and violence. Whenever the natural functions of life such as pulsation, vibration, flow, rhythm, opening and closing are hampered by moralistic or technical violence, malfunctions and illnesses result. This applies to nature in the outer world just as it applies to our inner nature; it applies to a river in the landscape as it does to love. If a meandering and freely vibrating river is locked into a straight bed of concrete, it is deprived of its natural self-healing powers. When Eros is locked into the straight concrete bed of sexual morals of the church or of matrimony, it too is deprived of its natural power to heal itself. Healing and becoming whole can start to take place as soon as our actions resonate with the functional principles of the living world. Biomorphism is a key word in discussing these ideas, which hold true outside as well as inside. SEXPEACE and GREENPEACE – peace between the genders and peace with nature. This is the framework in which the healing process toward a non-violent Earth can take place.

Structurally speaking there is no difference between violence against animals and violence against humans. Animals are humans like us. A cat's curiosity, its high spirit, its joy of life is the same as those of a child, only at a different level of evolution. What birds sing or chirp is an expression of their spirit and of their connection to this world. An animal's cry of pain is the same as that of a human in terms of its emotional and spiritual quality. The world is a community of living creatures imbued with spirits which communicate with one another and with the world as a whole in a certain way. All those creatures chirping, crawling, hopping and stretching are living beings just like us, only at a different stage of evolution, having been brought forth by a creation full of spirit, equipped with curiosity, with a will to live and with the ability to experience joy. The spiritual and mental energy lines of the Earth are not experienced exclusively by humans. They affect all creatures, at least in a rudimentary way. In all creatures there are basic qualities which we can characterize as either love or violence. Which of the two comes to expression, which of them comes to dominate real life, depends on the circumstances under which the individuals and the groups they form establish themselves. If we create circumstances based on violence, individual violence will result. If they are based on trust, then trust will result. The genetic code, the basic information of all life, permits either one to develop. Realizing this and taking advantage of it in a non-violent manner is the responsibility of every human being, for we are the eye of creation and the reflective organ with which it can look at itself. Today we have the capacity to recognize these interconnections, because they have formed us and we keep reproducing them in one way or another. We are the source of political, ecological and sexual violence. And this is exactly why we are also the source of the means to overcome it.

Overcoming structural violence means integrating the logic of creation and the logic of human beings. It means integrating both biological and cultural demands; in other words, the logic of organs and the logic of society must be integrated. If we want to overcome structural violence and replace it with structural love, we will have to transform our impulses and drives. Sexuality is divided into a permissible and a forbidden part, into partner sex and brothel sex, into fantasies that can be shown openly and others that have to be hidden. This double standard on every corner of our social structure is a major cause for the general distrust and structural violence we experience. We will only be able to overcome this traumatic basic structure if we learn to view our drives as they are and lift them into our conscious life without prejudging them. It is only by becoming aware of our drives, accepting and integrating them, that we will be able to liberate and humanize them in a controlled manner and be able to reflect upon and design the whole area of our sexuality in a new way without hatred or prejudice. Only when there are no more hidden explosive charges in our sexual attitudes and activities will we be able to start relying on each other. Trust and destruction do not go together. Love and trust are the authentic self-healing powers, for both nature and human beings. An organism that is touched by these powers usually heals itself. If our biosphere were filled with love and trust, it too would go through such a healing process. The creation of life systems in which the powers of trust and healing can grow is a research project of planetary importance.

The transformation of human culture from structural violence to the principle of structural non-violence is a very complex process which has an impact on all areas of life. It is not until we reach this truly comprehensive view that we will be able to assign new priorities and values to individual areas such as nutrition, recycling, energy, architecture, building materials, etc. It is very difficult to understand and elaborate on the concept of free love outside of this comprehensive perspective. Free love grows out of a profound understanding which is possible only in non-violent structures. Free love is closely linked to trust and truth, without which it has no meaning. Trust and truth, however, have long since disappeared from the list of basic human qualities in society; they will have to be recreated in new social spaces. For the realization of Greenpeace and Sexpeace we need Healing Biotopes in which both the sexual and the ecological dead-ends can be overcome. As pilot models for a non-violent culture these Healing Biotopes will be the natural points of crystallization for the development of new mental and spiritual realms.

While creating posters with a group of artists we once coined the statement, "In the search for sexual contact so much gasoline is consumed every day that the liberation of sexuality is necessary for purely ecological reasons if for no other." The idea expressed here can easily be applied to many areas of our current behavior of consumption and the consumer goods industry that goes with it. Most of this behavior serves only as a surrogate or replacement for the happiness of a love life that could never be attained. Let us imagine people living together without any fear, lies or distrust, without any obsolete restrictions that prevent them from experiencing love. We would lead awakened, sensual and creative lives. We would experience sexual fulfillment according to our own definition, without having to hide half of our desires. There would be sufficient intelligence and technical possibilities available for the adventure of research and development in all areas of the universe and the Earth. We would continuously discover new things in the fields of energy, nutrition, water, recycling. In short, we would lead fulfilled inner and outer lives and there would no longer be any need for vicarious experiences and surrogates for life.

Consider all the production of consumer goods, all the industrial devastation, all the waste of energy, water and raw materials that our Earth could thus be spared! So much of the destruction of our environment could be avoided if our inner world were sound. A life in community with others, with a fulfilled sexual life and creative pioneer work would replace the whole pharmaceutical industry! Once the inner forces of destruction have subsided, the remnants of the defense industry would be nothing more than rusty ruins rising up against the morning sky, slowly crumbling to dust.

The interconnections are clear. The current efforts being made to prevent an ecological catastrophe must be combined with even greater efforts aimed at solving the human issue. Ecological concepts must be supplemented by new concepts for love and community, otherwise neither perspective carries any conviction. The issue today is not whether or not we can do it, because we must do it.

Let me conclude this chapter by adding a few words about the very simple things I mean: Could a young man who has just made love to a young woman torture a rabbit? Could a leading member of a secret service force, who has found trust in mutual love, continue doing his job? Could the former president of East Germany have given the orders to fire if his body had been filled with love? Could a woman who has begun to understand the suffering of animals because of an experience of sensual love wear a fur coat? Could two people who have just made love on the beach pollute it with their garbage?

They could not, because they will have been transformed; they will have come to a point in their experience where the prevailing laws are different. You cannot destroy life if you yourself have just received it. Love and destruction will exclude each other once and for all as soon as a certain degree of consciousness has been attained. Liberated love between the genders, once it has been fully integrated, is tantamount to love for all of creation. May the same effort and commitment with which we are fighting for Greenpeace today be doubled in intensity for the realization of Sexpeace tomorrow.

A Home for Children

Adults too will find a home wherever children grow up to be happy. What sort of happiness is this? What is a child? What are the qualities that we should promote so that they become free and fulfilled human beings?

Maybe we should forget everything we ever learned about education and just open our eyes. The question of raising children is primarily a matter of perception; only secondarily is it a matter of education. We must realize that children need to be understood, not educated. Not until we see and understand can we begin to guide and support. This principle is neither authoritarian nor anti-authoritarian; it is simply the principle of participation, observation and recognition. Under these conditions children are able to find a home because they are understood and loved, which is not easy in this fast-paced, narcissistic world of ours.

Haven't we noticed how aware and alert children are, a trait which is already present within weeks of their birth? Haven't we been moved and even shocked by the keen attentiveness of their big eyes? Haven't we sensed the absolute presence of that spirit which is gazing into the world? We cannot apply our adult standards here, because the spiritual awareness and sense of identity that a child has is something we no longer possess since we have lost it in the monotony of our daily existence. This is the quintessential quality of children that we must cultivate and protect: their capacity for perception, wonder, curiosity and insight.

Children are intuitive and cognizant creatures at birth. When this is recognized and encouraged by their parents, the child's spiritual home begins to take form. The further mental and emotional development of the child depends on this.

By no means can we take for granted that parents love their children, especially when we consider the existing societal conditions. Often there is hardly any emotional link between the daily life of the parents and the child, which discovers the world from between the legs of adults. But it is just this awareness that the child requires in order to develop a deeper sense of love and security; it goes beyond changing emotional moods and whims. To love a child means to recognize its true nature. The same applies to any true love between human beings. When a child is loved in this sense, (s)he has found home, even if it is a little rough at times. If that is fulfilled, the child will demand no further proof of love, since (s)he has no fear of separation. This may be the basis of any true home: that we no longer need to fear separation and loss. Love without fear of separation.

Create home for children. Create structures of love and participation where children can once again trust their parents. Where there is trust, there is home for every creature. We ourselves, we adults, would like to learn how to discover the world in the same way as children do, as if for the first time, as something completely new and unspoiled. A child learns its mother tongue without having to memorize one single word. There is so much that we adults can learn once we have rediscovered time, peace and joy in life. Whenever we create a home for children, we create one for ourselves as well.

Eros Redeemed

Imagine waking up one morning with the realization that there is no fear or hatred within you any more. You recall the usual worries of the last few years, but you no longer have any. The past is within you in the form of a treasure of experiences and knowledge, but no longer as an emotion or a source of pain. You recall your friends and relationships and your happy and unhappy experiences, but you don't need to get down on yourself for anything, because nothing is threatening you any more. You see your former lovers as you did at the time when you were in love with them and you realize that you are basically still in love with them. You would be happy to meet them again, since all complications of fear, guilt, justifications and all fights you had are a thing of the past. You remember and know exactly what happened, but in your spirit and body there is no fear left and no hatred either, since hatred only resulted from fear. You see these correlations clearly, but you do not dwell on them, for there are no problems left to be explained or solved. The rising sun meets you above the mists of your previous entanglements. You are now filled with this bright world, which has remained intact up to this day. You are so filled with a wordless feeling of gratitude and love that even the cigarette, which you normally would have reached for, seems strange to you. You have the feeling that you know this state of perfect health and it's wonderful that it has returned after all these decades of painful struggle.

These are the moments in life when the vision of a different mode of existence comes shining through our lives so concretely and realistically that we can't just go on with daily work. This experience is reality. Beyond all of this disintegration there exists a life without fear, a state of grace through love. The universe is organized in such a way that this possibility lies open to us. All those who have experienced this state of being can bear witness to it. There is a state of awareness in which all things appear as gifts. I go down to my morning bistro and order a cup of coffee. Normally I wouldn't notice the waitress, but now I do. It is a joy to greet her; it is a joy to sit in this room. Here, simple human contact is made with no effort at all, and it is not difficult to imagine how it could continue into the bustle of the day. Where there is no fear, there is no restless yearning either, no needs of the old kind and no need for constant emotional reactions. You radiate something that protects you, and this protection enables you to act with a lightness that overcomes all barriers. This also goes for the most attractive representatives of the opposite sex. Pure joy arises if there is no more fear and no barriers. What problems we created in the past when it came to making erotic contacts! Now it happens all by itself. There is an Asian proverb that says: Difficulties are overcome through lightness. If lightness is applied, the difficulties disappear, and the world reveals its true possibilities. Difficulties are always connected to some sort of heaviness, and we are heavy when we are stuck in the corresponding energy. But now, when these energies have left us, we stand safe and steady outside of this world of projections. We have no reason for fear, for we are protected; we also do not have a reason for anger, for we do not judge when we are in a state of love. We have no cause for wrath, for we have the freedom to act without fear. If now I am attracted to a woman, then I am sure I will know what to do. And if at first she rejects me out of fear, then I can accept her reaction without taking it personally. I don't need to invent any excuses or justifications. I would simply like to tell her that she is sexually attractive to me, that's all. I know very well that there is nothing she would like to hear more than that. But I can continue to live in good health even if she says no. Maybe it'll work out later. I don't have to react emotionally to her rejection, because behind it I can see her own situation, her secret desire and her expectations. She is like me, only the other way around. Just like me, she needs a situation of lightness and ease in which to accept my offer with joy. I pick a daisy and put it in her décolleté.

Have you ever gone out on the pier of a harbor in the evening and met a woman who was as alone as you? Isn't it strange, in such a situation, just to pass each other by without saying a word? Doesn't it leave you with a bad feeling, almost a feeling of guilt? If the world were different, wouldn't you have gone up next to her to look out at the sea together? And if then, embracing the elements, you were to follow the naturalness of Eros, and if she didn't have a man who was warily waiting for her in the next bar, would you have to regret such a contact afterwards? Couldn't this whole world be a love affair if it weren't so confined by our cowardly rules? Couldn't many men and women look out into the world with happier eyes if such contacts were more natural and more normal? The woman with the nice figure who is lying there alone on her deck chair – what is she thinking about? Can't I call over to her and ask her if there is any wish I can fulfill for her? Redeemed Eros thrives on such small gestures. Am I only allowed to pay when I pass the woman at the cash register in the supermarket? Must I always suppress my tendency to notice her neck and her breasts? Of course it's not necessarily a matter of going to bed with her; it is a matter of getting rid of the inner barriers that prevent any real human and sensuous contact. Everywhere, everywhere. We have gotten so used to secrecy that we hardly notice it any more. We are creating appearances that keep us from living and from loving. We live in a world of pretense.

The redemption of Eros naturally means showing your sexual interest. The more naturally this occurs, the more authentic we become. And the more authentic we become, the more identical we become with ourselves and the less fear we create in others.

Here I would like to add a thought to the chapter about Eros and religion. We have emerged from a fog of constrictions and fear and we look into another world. We look into a world from which no threat is felt. It is a joyful surprise to see this world again. With gratitude we realize the naturalness of how easily things work. There are loving people who have no fences or masks around them. How friendly they greet you. A world that is free from fences is a love affair. There is not the slightest doubt about the reality of this perception. It is like waking up after a long nightmare. We are amazed at that reduction of life which in the old structures of isolation and jealousy we called "normal." This kind of revelation is like a miracle; the believable thing about it is that we already know it somewhere inside ourselves. Having woken up to a greater potential of existence, we see thoughts and images that are as familiar to us as our very own.

There is no greater longing and no greater love than that between the genders. And these genders, men and women, meet everywhere. But in the world of unredeemed Eros they are forced to act as if nothing were there. In reality everything is there. Always and everywhere, it's omnipresent, the whole issue. It doesn't start only when we have found a woman or man for life, and it doesn't stop there either. As long as human beings are divided into men and women, the issue of sexual attraction will always be the most important human issue. In the name of love, we have to accept the fact that we are sexual beings. In the name of love, we have the task of freeing sexuality from all rubbish and all cruelty so that it can become what it is meant to be: the joy that the genders take in each other and the resurrection of love on our planet.

In the name of warmth for all creatures and in the name of all children.

Recommended Literature

Bach, Richard. Jonathan Livingston Seagull. New York: Macmillan, 1970. Print.

Bataille, Georges. The Tears of Eros. San Francisco: City Lights, 1989. Print.

Bloch, Ernst. The Principle of Hope. Cambridge, MA: MIT, 1996. Print.

Chardin, Pierre Teilhard De, Julian Huxley, and Bernard Wall. The Phenomenon of Man. New York: Harper, 1959. Print.

Daimler, Renate. Verschwiegene Lust: Frauen über 60 erzählen von Liebe und Sexualität. Köln: Kiepenheuer & Witsch, 1991. Print.

Deschner, Karlheinz. Kriminalgeschichte des Christentums. Reinbek Bei Hamburg: Rowohlt, 1986. Print.

Duhm, Dieter. Politische Texte für eine gewaltfreie Erde. Belzig: Verlag Meiga, 1992. Print.

Duhm, Dieter. Towards a New Culture. Belzig: Verlag Meiga, 2012. Print.

Duhm, Dieter. The Sacred Matrix: From the Matrix of Violence to the Matrix of Life; the Foundation for a New Civilization. Wiesenburg: Verlag Meiga, 2006. Print.

Duhm, Dieter, and Madjana Geusen. Man's Holy Grail Is Woman Paintings, Drawings and Texts. Wiesenburg: Verlag Meiga, 2006. Print.

Duhm, Dieter. Future without War: Theory of Global Healing. Wiesenburg: Verlag Meiga, 2007. Print.

Eisler, Riane Tennenhaus. The Chalice and the Blade: Our History, Our Future. Cambridge: Harper & Row, 1987. Print.

Emmermann, Heide-Marie. Credo an Gott und sein Fleisch: Erfahrungen mit irdischer und himmlischer Liebe. Hamburg: Hoffmann und Campe, 1991. Print.

Ghazal, Eluan. Schlangenkult Und Tempelliebe: Sakrale Erotik in archaischen Gesellschaften. Berlin: Simon Leutner, 1995. Print.

Goethe, Johann Wolfgang Von. The Sorrows of Young Werther: Die Leiden Des Jungen Werther. Mineola, NY: Dover Publications, 2004. Print.

Jong, Erica. Fear of Flying: A Novel. New York: Holt, Rinehart and Winston, 1973. Print.

Kleinhammes, Sabine. Rettet Den Sex: Ein Manifest von Frauen für einen neuen sexuellen Humanismus. Belzig:Verlag Meiga, 1988. Print.

Lichtenfels, Sabine. Grace: Pilgrimage for a Future without War. Wiesenburg: Verlag Meiga, 2007. Print.

Lichtenfels, Sabine. Sources of Love and Peace. Belzig: Verl. Meiga, 2004. Print.

Lichtenfels, Sabine. Traumsteine: Reise in das Zeitalter der sinnlichen Erfüllung. Muenchen: Hugendubel, 2000. Print.

Lichtenfels, Sabine. Weiche Macht: Perspektiven eines neuen Frauenbewusstseins und einer neuen Liebe zu den Männern. Belzig,:Verlag Meiga, 1996. Print.

Meulenbelt, Anja. The Shame Is Over: A Political Life Story. London: Women's, 1980. Print.

Miller, Alice. Breaking down the Wall of Silence: The Liberating Experience of Facing Painful Truth. New York, NY, U.S.A.: Dutton, 1991. Print.

Miller, Henry. The Colossus of Maroussi. New York: New Directions, 1958. Print.

Miller, Henry. Opus Pistorum. New York: Grove, 1983. Print.

Möller, Beate. Die Heilige und die Hure: Bilder und Texte einer Ausstellung. Belzig: Verlag Meiga, 1989. Print.

Mulford, Prentice. The Use and Necessity of Recreation. Whitefish, MT: Kessinger, 2005. Print.

Nin, Anaïs. Delta of Venus. London: Penguin, 2000. Print.

Reich, Wilhelm. The Function of the Orgasm; Sex-economic Problems of Biological Energy. New York: Farrar, Straus and Giroux, 1973. Print.

Reich, Wilhelm. The Cancer Biopathy. New York: Farrar, Straus and Giroux, 1973. Print.

Schubart, Walter. Religion und Eros. Muenchen: C.H. Beck, 1966. Print.

Satprem. Sri Aurobindo: Or, The Adventure of Consciousness. New York: Harper & Row, 1968. Print.

Schwenk, Theodor. Sensitive Chaos: The Creation of Flowing Forms in Water and Air. New York: Schocken, 1976. Print.

Zorn, Fritz. Mars. New York: Knopf, 1982. Print.

Further Information:

The thoughts described in this book are part of a complex vision based on over 30 years of research. In 1995, four years after the original German version of this book was published, the author founded the Peace Research Center Tamera in Portugal together with his partner the theologian Sabine Lichtenfels and others. In this context the vision could start to take form and substance. Today an ever-growing team of highly committed people is working in Tamera and in some other parts of the world to realize this peace vision which in its core is to be based on trust between the genders. Sustainable funding is urgently needed. Please refer to the website www.the-grace-foundation.org for detailed information. Whoever is willing to support, please donate to:

Tamera:

Account Holder: Associação para um mundo humanitário Bank:
Caixa Crédito Agrícola S. Teotónio, Portugal
NIB: 0045 6332 4018 1786 5584 5
IBAN: PT50 0045 6332 4018 1786 5584 5
BIC: CCCMPTPL

GRACE Foundation:

Raiffeisenbank Zurich

Account Holder: Grace Foundation for the Humanization of Money, Zurich
Account Number: 92188.69 • IBAN: CH9881487000009218869
BIC: RAIFCH22 • Clearing 81487
(PC-Account of the bank: 87-71996-7)
Paypal/credit card:
You can donate via Paypal or credit card through our website:
www.the-grace-foundation.org

Contact:

Institute for Global Peace Work (IGP)
Monte do Cerro • 7630-303 Colos, • Portugal
Tel. (+351) 283 635 484 • igp@tamera.org • www.tamera.org

Thank you!

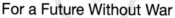

VERLAG MEIGA
For a Future Without War

Dieter Duhm
The Sacred Matrix
From the Matrix of Violence to the Matrix of Life
ISBN: 978-3-927266-16-2

Dieter Duhm
Future without War
Theory of Global Healing
ISBN: 978-3-927266-24-7

Sabine Lichtenfels
GRACE
Pilgrimage for a Future without War
ISBN: 978-3-927266-25-4

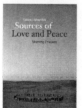

Sabine Lichtenfels
Sources of Love and Peace
Morning Prayers
ISBN: 978-3-927266-11-7

www.verlag-meiga.org

CPSIA information can be obtained
at www.ICGtesting.com
Printed in the USA
FSOW02n1911110416
19037FS